Letter From The Founder

CINDY WITTEMAN
Founder & CEO

Welcome to the latest edition of Force Magazine, a passion project close to my heart. Here, we shine a spotlight on the remarkable deeds of everyday heroes. In a world often overshadowed by negativity, this magazine is a reminder of the good that exists.

Within these pages, you'll meet individuals who not only excel in their businesses but also find ways to give back, making the world a better place, one act of kindness at a time. Their stories never fail to inspire me, and I hope they do the same for you.

As the founder and CEO, I feel privileged to share these stories with you. They fuel my belief in the power of compassion and the difference it can make in the world. Thank you for joining us on this journey of hope and positivity.

Let's spread kindness and positivity together,

Cindy Witteman
Founder & CEO
Force Magazine

My Business: CF Views LLC - CFViews.com (Owner)
Little Give - TV Show - LittleGive.com (Host)
Non-Profit: Driving Single Parents Inc. - DrivingSingleParents.org
(Founder & CEO)

THE POWER OF TRANSFORMATION: HOW TO TURN YOUR PAIN INTO PURPOSE

by Jennifer Perri

Life is a journey filled with peaks and valleys, and for many, it can seem like the valleys stretch endlessly, casting shadows of despair and hopelessness. However, within these darkest moments lies the potential for profound transformation—a transformation that can turn pain into purpose, despair into hope, and adversity into resilience. Jennifer Perri, a Transformational Life and Empowerment Coach, has walked this path herself, and through her experiences, she has guided countless others on their journeys of turning trials into triumphs.

From Darkness to Light: The Beginning of the Journey

Jennifer's life has been a testament to the power of transformation. Her journey from a top student in high school, filled with dreams and ambition, to a young woman caught in the grips of an abusive first marriage, was the first of many trials she would face. Like many young women, Jennifer believed that a loving marriage and motherhood would be a natural path at some point in her life. But life had other plans. The man who vowed to love and protect her became her abuser, isolating her from friends and family, trapping her in a cycle of fear and control.

The pain and terror she endured were not just a series of unfortunate events but a grueling training ground for the challenges she would face later in life. However, Jennifer's story is not one of victimhood but of victory. Escaping her first marriage was only the first step; the journey to reclaim her life was far more daunting.

Breaking Free and Rebuilding

Leaving an abusive relationship is a monumental step, but it is also the beginning of a long and arduous journey. Jennifer found herself in uncharted territory, with no roadmap to navigate the path back to normalcy. Unlike her peers, who were building careers and pursuing higher education, Jennifer was a young mother struggling to survive and provide for her children.

In her late twenties, Jennifer re-entered the workforce, initially out of necessity, but soon with a newfound determination to become someone of significance. She chose the field of finance, driven by a desire to help women like herself—women who had been through trauma and needed to regain control over their lives. Her experiences with abuse, divorce, single parenting, and remarriage became the foundation of a successful financial consulting career, where she empowered others to find stability and security.

The Healing Process: Understanding and Overcoming Trauma

The journey of transformation is not a straight path; it is filled with twists, turns, and moments of deep introspection. For Jennifer, the healing process began when she started to reflect on her past, asking herself, "Why did this happen to me?" and "Did I do something to deserve this?" It was during this time that she was diagnosed with complex PTSD, a result of the years of violence she had endured.

This diagnosis brought clarity and understanding to the fog she had been living in. It explained the years she spent feeling trapped, even after escaping her abusive marriage. True healing began when Jennifer found the right support—a husband who stood by her side and a trauma expert who had walked a similar path. For the first time, Jennifer felt truly understood, and this connection allowed her to start rebuilding the broken pieces of her life.

Jennifer embraced the process of self-love, creating vision boards, and daily affirmations to rebuild her shattered self-esteem. This journey of healing was not just about overcoming past trauma but about discovering a new sense of purpose and direction in life.

A New Beginning: From Financial Consultant to Transformational Coach

Jennifer's experiences and the resilience she developed through her struggles naturally led her to a new calling—transformational coaching. She realized that her true purpose was not just in helping women become financially stable but in empowering them to reclaim their lives, just as she had done.

Inspired by her childhood role model, Wonder Woman, Jennifer founded SHERO Life & Empowerment Coaching. The essence of SHERO was to help women discover their inner superheroes, to tap into their potential, and to rewrite their life stories with courage, resilience, and heart. Through SHERO, Jennifer aimed to inspire and guide others on their empowering journeys, much like Wonder Woman had inspired her.

Another Mountain to Climb: The Battle with Guillain-Barre Syndrome

Just when Jennifer thought she was on a steady path of recovery and empowerment, life threw another challenge her way. In December 2021, she was diagnosed with Guillain-Barre Syndrome (GBS), a rare neurological disorder that left her paralyzed and facing an uncertain future. The prognosis was grim, with doctors estimating it might take at least a year before she could walk again.

The hospital became Jennifer's new battleground, where she fought for every inch of progress. The support of her family, especially her husband, Carmine, became her pillars of strength during this difficult time. Despite the pain, fear, and uncertainty, Jennifer refused to surrender to bitterness. She chose to fight, determined to get better and reclaim her life once more.

Finding Strength in Vulnerability and Resilience

After a month in the hospital and intensive therapy, Jennifer was finally allowed to return home, although still confined to a wheelchair. But she was far from defeated. At the age of 50, she began the arduous process of relearning basic tasks, including walking, writing, and dressing herself. In what can only be described as a miracle, Jennifer took her first steps just 56 days later, surpassing all expectations.

Jennifer's battle with GBS became a mirror reflecting the resilience she had been building all her life. Every day was a test of will, but with each small victory, she found new purpose and strength. Her journey through GBS taught her to find blessings in chaos and gratitude in the smallest of things.

Transforming Adversity into Opportunity: The Birth of the Empowerment Blueprint

Jennifer's struggle with GBS was not just a personal battle; it was a lesson in transforming adversity into opportunity. This experience deepened her commitment to helping other women facing their own battles. She realized that her journey had equipped her with unique insights and tools that could benefit a broader audience.

Driven by this newfound purpose, Jennifer transitioned from one-on-one coaching to developing a more comprehensive program—The Empowerment Blueprint™. This program was designed to provide women with the tools they needed to navigate life's challenges and emerge stronger, more confident, and empowered.

The Empowerment Blueprint is built around the C.A.P.E. Method, which focuses on four critical areas: Clarity & Confidence, Alignment & Authenticity, Passion & Purpose, and Empowered to Live Extraordinary.

Clarity & Confidence: Jennifer helps women gain clarity on their true desires and builds their confidence to pursue them.

Alignment & Authenticity: This phase focuses on aligning daily actions with core values and beliefs, fostering a life lived with purpose and unapologetic authenticity.

Passion & Purpose: Jennifer guides women in identifying their passions and integrating them into their lives, leading to deeper fulfillment and sustainable happiness.

Empowered to Live Extraordinary: The final stage involves creating a comprehensive action plan to achieve goals, ensuring that women are equipped with the tools and mindset to succeed and live a truly epic life.

The Outcome: A Life of Purpose and Fulfillment

The goal of transformation, as Jennifer Perri teaches, is to live a life of purpose and fulfillment. This does not mean a life free of pain or challenges, but rather a life in which those challenges are met with strength, resilience, and a deep sense of purpose.

When individuals embrace their pain, shift their perspective, and find purpose in their experiences, they can live more authentically and intentionally. They are no longer defined by their past, but by the purpose they have discovered through it. This sense of purpose brings fulfillment, as individuals feel that their lives have meaning and that they are making a positive impact on the world.

Jennifer often shares stories of her clients who have undergone profound transformations, turning their pain into powerful platforms for change. These individuals have not only healed from their pasts but have also used their experiences to inspire and uplift others.

Embrace the Power of Transformation

Jennifer Perri's life is a living testament to the power of transformation. Her journey, though filled with hardships, has led her to a place of strength, purpose, and a deep desire to help others overcome their own challenges. Through her courses, books and speaking opportunities, Jennifer continues to guide women on their paths from pain to purpose, showing them that within every trial lies the potential for profound growth and empowerment.

Transformation is not an easy process, but it is one of the most rewarding journeys a person can undertake. By facing their pain, learning from it, and using it as a catalyst for growth, individuals can create lives that are not only fulfilling but also deeply impactful. As Jennifer often says, "Your pain is your power. Use it to transform yourself and the world around you."

Connect With Jennifer

www.JenniferPerri.com

Taking Responsibility for What Shows Up in Your Life
A PATH TO EMPOWERMENT AND GROWTH

By Lainne Love

Isn't it interesting to think about how truly wondrous your life is? You are an eternal soul having a human experience. God only knows how many lives and experiences went into weaving the intricate tapestry of your life as it is today, each thread representing a choice, a belief, or an action that contributed to the dynamic picture of your existence.

Understanding and embracing the choice to take responsibility for what shows up in your life is not about assigning blame or guilt. It's about recognizing your ability to influence and shape reality through your choices and actions, empowering you to transform challenges into opportunities and to actively participate in creating a life that aligns with your deepest desires and values. As well as interweaves the many parts of who you are now and who you have been in other lifetimes and realities.

The Empowerment of Responsibility

Taking responsibility for what shows up in your life is about choice and power, acknowledging that while the jury may still be out on who or what controls every external circumstance, ultimately, you have the power to choose your response to circumstances or events in ways that align with your goals and vision. This shift in perspective is crucial because it moves you from a passive position of being affected by life to an active role in shaping it.

When you take responsibility, you are declaring that you are not merely a spectator in your own life but the primary architect of your experience participating in creating your divine blueprint. This empowering act is incredibly liberating, placing control and agency firmly in your hands.

Shifting from Blame to Ownership

When things don't go as planned, it's easy to fall into the trap of blaming external factors or other people, I know have. Let's face it, even on the best days, do things ever go as planned? Now I aim to have things turn out even better than I imagined and intentionally leave room for surprises. While it's natural to feel frustration when faced with challenges, shifting from blame to ownership is a powerful step towards shaping the best version of yourself.

I teach my clients to shift by learning to start asking themselves questions, "What can I learn from this situation?" and "How is this happening for me?" This shift allows you to see opportunities by turning obstacles into learning experiences and taking proactive steps toward possibility.

Embracing the Lessons in Challenges

Every challenge is an opportunity for growth and self-discovery. Challenges are providing the next steps that you need to take; they are leading you in the direction to develop the skillset you need to achieve your goal. By taking responsibility, you open yourself up to the lessons that these challenges offer. For example, if a project at work doesn't go as planned, learn to shift and to look for the clue, the opportunity, and what you can learn from the experience. Perhaps there are areas where you can improve your skills or communication.

Cultivating an Expansion Mindset

When you invest in choosing a growth mindset/expansion mindset, you view challenges and setbacks as part of the learning process rather than as indicators of failure. You'll learn to see every experience —whether positive or negative—as a chance to improve and evolve. This perspective encourages you to embrace new challenges, seek feedback, and persist undeterred by adversity, all of which contribute to your overall development and success.

The Role of Self-Awareness

Self-awareness involves understanding your thoughts, emotions, and behaviors and how they influence your experiences, it will help you identify patterns in your life and make more conscious choices. You can develop self-awareness by pausing to reflect on your responses to various situations. What do you notice? Are there recurring patterns in your reactions? Are you reacting when you want to be responding? Are there certain triggers that consistently lead to negative outcomes? By becoming more aware of your patterns, you can make more informed choices and address the underlying issues affecting your life.

Journaling, meditation, seeking feedback from trusted friends or mentors, and reviewing your day can be valuable tools for developing self-awareness. These practices allow you to gain insights into your behavior and make adjustments that align with your goals and vision. I ask my clients to write down what they are proud of themselves for and what they could have improved on each day, this is a great way to notice what is working and what isn't. It's just as important to notice and celebrate what is working as it is to notice what needs improvement.

Setting Intentions and Goals

Taking responsibility also involves setting clear intentions and goals for yourself. When you have a clear vision of what you want to achieve, you direct your actions, energy, and decisions toward that vision. This clarity helps you stay focused and motivated. Break down your goals into actionable steps and create a plan. Review your progress and adjust your strategies as needed. By taking responsibility for your goals and actively working towards them, you create a sense of purpose and direction in your life.

Building a Support System

Surround yourself with people who encourage and inspire you. These individuals can provide valuable support, feedback, and perspective as you work towards creating the life you want.
Seek mentors, friends, and colleagues who share your values and aspirations. Engage in communities or groups that align with your interests and goals. Investing in and nurturing a strong support system provides motivation, accountability, and encouragement, making taking responsibility more enjoyable and rewarding.

Practicing Self-Compassion

Taking responsibility doesn't mean being unkind or critical of yourself. Practicing self-compassion and recognizing that mistakes and setbacks are a natural part of the process is an important part of the journey.
By being gentle with yourself, you create a supportive inner environment that encourages you to keep moving forward and striving for your goals.

Connect With Lainne

www.lainne.com
www.linkedin.com/in/lainnelove
www.instagram.com/lainnelove
www.facebook.com/lainnelove

Celebrating Your Successes

Reflect on your progress and recognize how far you have come. Celebrate your successes, no matter how small they may seem. Acknowledging and celebrating your achievements reinforces your sense of accomplishment and motivation.

Final Thoughts

Remember, that you are the architect of your experience. Each choice you make weaves another thread into the tapestry of your life leaving its mark behind, sometimes its light, sometimes its shadow. No matter the shade each experience has its value and place. Taking responsibility for what shows up in your life is transformative, life-changing and will lead to greater fulfillment. By shifting from blame to ownership, embracing challenges as opportunities, cultivating a growth mindset, and practicing self-awareness, you are actively shaping your reality and creating your life with intention.

MARY ANN STENQUIST

One of the biggest myths is that there are only two types of people when it comes to money: spenders and savers. The often referenced two sides of the coin, 'Savers' and 'Spenders' is an inaccurate and often misleading identification for someone's behavior with money. The focus of these terms is on what you buy, not why. What we need to ask is, why does someone feel the need to save and not buy? Why do others feel the need to spend and not save? Even people that don't spend money have a reason for why they don't spend money. It all comes down to the psychology of spending.

Mary Ann, a Spending Coach and creator of Become Unshoppable, identified six Spending Types or spending habits that represent what drives us to spend, so that we can stop spending before it happens. Her approach involves getting to the root cause of overspending so we can overcome the urge to shop and become unshoppable.

The purpose of Become Unshoppable is a mission dedicated to helping people end overspending so they can be guilt-free, debt-free, and experience true financial freedom. But first, what does it mean to be unshoppable?

"It's about not letting your life be consumed by consumerism." Mary Ann has experienced firsthand the strangling hold of consumerism.
She was shopping daily—and when she wasn't out shopping, she was shopping on her phone for her next big purchase. It consumed her thoughts, actions, and her life.

But the answer to fix her spending addiction did not come easy. In her search for answers, the only actionable advice was to make a budget. While traditional budgets may encourage saving and decreased spending, they don't give you active tools to address spending habits. She states, "With a budget, you are looking at money before you've had a chance to spend it and after it's been spent. That doesn't address the underlying spending habits."

What makes Mary Ann's approach so unique is looking at the root cause of our spending behaviors. "There is a psychological reason behind why we buy that nobody talks about, and yet it's key to stopping habits of overspending."

Unable to find answers, she was forced to forge her own path. She decided to look at her spending to see where the money was going. This led to the realization that outside of bills and fixed expenses, her habits of overspending totaled to over a thousand dollars every month.

"I started to see trends and patterns emerge in my spending: all the times I bought bargains to steal the deal or all the times I bought to make myself feel better. Seeing these patterns in my spending made me wonder, were these spending trends unique to me, or were they applicable to all people that struggle with overspending?"

Her spending analysis led to the identification of six main spending habits that represent what drives our urge to spend, what she calls the Six Spending Types.

The Necessity Spender overspends most on items that are needed for the household and for family members and close friends. This spending archetype is often considered our 'savers,' but it's really those that don't like to spend a lot of money. For the Necessity Spender, they crave safety and security; and that need is much more appealing than the occasional wanted item. However, even necessities can be a source of overspending. Yes, you need trail mix because your kids eat it after school. But do you really need 10 bags of trail mix? Or are you stocking up to meet your need for security and stocking up on all the items you use to fill that need?

The Bargain Spender spends most of their money on bargains. For them, it is the price of the item that determines the purchase. But bargains can be a huge source of overspending. If you buy something you don't need, you lose money—no matter how much you save. The focus needs to be on what you spend, not just how much you saved. Ask yourself, do you really need that item right now or are you just afraid to miss out on the deal?

The Emotional Spender overspends most during times of heightened emotions, both positive and negative. This type of spender often turns to shopping to replace undesired emotions with more positive emotions. They are driven to buy items to meet the need for love and belonging and for esteem. They may feel they can earn respect through material items. We think that it's the material things that give us self-esteem, but they can actually keep us from achieving it ourselves—from within us.

The Impulsive Spender spends most of their money on items that were not planned for in advance. While the price can persuade the Impulsive Spender to buy, it is usually an item that is one-of-a-kind, low-in-stock, or one tha thas unique features. Ultimately it's the fear of letting it slip away, or the fear of 'not having it if they need it' that finalizes the purchase. Other triggers to buy can be the latest trends as the Impulsive Spender craves inclusion and wants to belong with the crowd by owning similar things.

The Passive Spender is not actively aware of the use of their money—meaning they underestimate how much they spend and overestimate the funds they have available to spend. For them, the desire to spend money on an experience or an item is more valuable than the money. In other words, they will choose spending over saving every time. It is important to find what one values most, to help direct whimsical spending decisions to value-based decisions.

Although we all go through periods of spending and saving, the Saving Spender goes through cycles of spending and saving. These patterns can be seen when cycles of saving usually follow periods of overspending, and periods of spending follow a time of saving in repeatable patterns.

Once you have identified what drives your urge to overspend, you can begin to take steps to stop spending. And that is the foundation of Become Unshoppable. Becoming Unshoppable is realizing that items of consumption cannot actually bring us what we need. We often use material to fill inner voids; voids that cannot be filled with consumption. We have to recognize what we are trying to buy, or what need we are trying to fill with our purchases.

WHAT'S YOUR

Spending Type?

TAKE THE QUIZ

Connect With Mary Ann

maryann@becomeunshoppable.com
www.facebook.com/groups/431768277491464
www.instagram.com/becomeunshoppable
www.linkedin.com/in/mary-ann-stenquist

Necessity Spender

Saving Spender

The Spending Types

Bargain Spender

Passive Spender

Impulsive Spender

Emotional Spender

Living the the principles that she teaches in her signature course, Become Unshoppable, Mary Ann's life has been forever changed. "I can now walk out of my favorite stores without bags of purchases. I don't have to hide the evidence of my 'quick errand' that was really a trip to the mall. In fact, I no longer dread financial discussions with my husband because I am no longer overspending. For the first time I feel in control of my spending—and that feeling is priceless."

So the question to ask yourself isn't whether you are a spender or a saver, it's: what's your Spending Type? Take the Spending Type Quiz today to discover your Spending Type so that you, too, can become unshoppable.

FROM MENTALLY WELL TO MENTALLY WEALTHY

By Travis Lee

In the fast-paced, energetic world of entrepreneurship, it can often be easy to get caught up in the numbers game. Chasing sales, clients, business growth, and the beautifully displayed results plastered all over social media. Many entrepreneurs find themselves burnt out even in the midst of success because they forget to acknowledge a very important aspect of the lifestyle: taking care of their inner selves and developing a standard for mental wellness.

While monetary wealth is a great thing to have, the concept of mental wealth has the ability to completely change the entrepreneurial landscape. Imagine a community of entrepreneurs well-equipped and armored with the tools to not only properly address their own mental wellness but create a solid foundation in their business ventures where they can effectively communicate and exercise transparency in their challenges to deepen professional connections.

Mental wealth goes beyond the traditional concept of mental health. It's not just about avoiding burnout or managing stress; it's about thriving. It's the state of having a rich inner life, characterized by strong self-awareness, resilience, and emotional intelligence. For entrepreneurs, this can translate into better decision-making, improved leadership, and a more sustainable approach to business growth.

Mental wealth involves regular practices that nurture the mind, such as mindfulness, meditation, physical exercise, and continual learning. These practices help build a reservoir of inner strength that entrepreneurs can draw upon during challenging times.

The entrepreneurial world is beginning to recognize the importance of mental wealth. As more entrepreneurs share their journeys and the positive impact of focusing on mental wealth, a new paradigm is emerging. This shift is not just about creating successful businesses but building a sustainable and fulfilling entrepreneurial life.

Entrepreneurs are now looking beyond the traditional metrics of success. They are realizing that true wealth encompasses not only financial success but also a rich and fulfilling inner life. By prioritizing mental wealth, they are setting a new standard for what it means to be successful and build a legacy.

Mental wealth might just be next frontier in the world of entrepreneurship. By nurturing their minds and building a strong foundation of mental wellness, entrepreneurs can achieve greater creativity, better decision-making, stronger relationships, and resilience. This holistic approach to success is not just beneficial for their businesses but also for their overall well-being. The journey from being mentally well to mentally wealthy is one that can transform the entrepreneurial landscape, creating a community of thriving, innovative, and fulfilled individuals.

Connect with Travis

www.facebook.com/profile.php?id=100089867931671

www.linkedin.com/in/travis-lee

Email: AspyreLyfe@gmail.com

Phone: (503)926-9527

GET FEATURED!
GET IN FRONT OF READERS WORLDWIDE

BECOME A FORCE *today*

VISIT CFVIEWS.COM

SCAN THE QR CODE TO LEARN MORE

BUSINESS GROWTH CAN BE ELEGANTLY SIMPLE WRITTEN BY CHRISTINE CAMPBELL RAPIN

As an online business owner, it sometimes feels that everyone else is having epic $100K launches or crushing $10K+ months effortlessly while you struggle to attract clients consistently. This can lead to comparison and spirals of self-doubt about whether your business dreams are achievable. Let's bring a much-needed dose of reality to the topic client growth. Consistent client growth becomes possible when you understand the foundation from which every successful business is built and learn to build them in your own business.

Despite the highlight reel which is making you feel crappy about your business results, don't believe the hype. The truth is that less than 12% of female business owners are making more than 6 figures in their business and only about 2% are making 7 figures and there is much opportunity to improve those statistics.

As a business mentor who has worked with more than 400 companies to create over a billion dollars in combined revenue, we know that business growth CAN be elegantly simple (it will never be effortless). Everyone's dreams are different, be sure you are pursuing your own version of success.

To create success, building a profitable business with predictable client growth requires focused effort. Whether you are a solopreneur or have a team in your business, to achieve consistent client growth there are 3 daily non-negotiables to focus on:

1. Build an audience of buyers (note I didn't say followers.)

2. Master your marketing message to be able to move a potential buyer from being curious about your programs and services to being a paying client.

3. Make offers to potential buyers that create highly valued results more predictably than the current method they are using.

What many business owners don't understand when they first launch their business is that their business growth will be built on strangers. This simple reality is why audience building is THE most important business foundation.

Those aspirational $100K launches and $10K+ months only become possible once you have built an audience of buyers. Unfortunately, many business owners don't know how to build an audience of buyers or neglect to make this a critical area of focus throughout the life of the business and feel overwhelmed by the complexity of trying to do a million different things and not seeing the desired results.

Learning who you want to serve, selecting and executing the strategies that you will use to attract potential buyers to help them discover you, knowing why they would choose to invest in you and having the confidence to make right offer at the right time that focuses on desired outcomes and results are key skills every business owner needs to develop and master.

Even when you have a strong pipeline of potential buyers in your audience, you still need to spend 50% of your effort on this critical activity. When you are starting out and building awareness of why you are the must-hire choice to a particular group of potential buyers, this needs to be your single biggest area of daily focus (roughly 70-80% of your time).

To achieve this level of focus without burnout, stop the busy work that isn't leading you to successfully identifying new potential buyers and having offers accepted.

Potential buyers have 3 key attributes:

1. They are problem aware.

2. They are actively seeking solutions and support to reach their desired results or outcomes.

3. They have made the commitment to prioritize seeking support and taking different actions to create their desired results because their current strategy is no longer effective.

Too often business owners make the mistake of focusing on educating non-buyers on why they should be buyers, and this leads to frustration and often non-existent sales. Remember that the fastest path to cash is to go where the market is already seeking a solution and position yourself as the must-hire expert of choice.

Be aware that buyers do not want to pay for your time. They are willing to pay for the RESULTS they seek. Your programs and services need to be viewed as a predictable way to achieve results utilizing less time and money than their next best alternative. For them to choose you specifically as the must-hire expert to guide and support them, you need to establish:

• Trust that you have personal experience and know how to create the results they seek.

• Trust that you can guide them to create the results they seek for themselves

• Trust that they can be vulnerable with you with their current situation, knowledge gaps and that you will stick by them and follow through with your commitment to creating results together.

Once a potential buyer is aware of you, views you as the must-hire expert to guide and support them to achieve their desired results, you must be ready to make an offer that delivers predictable highly valued results.

Clients seek out and desire high touch experiences that lead to measurable results both short and long term. Be intentional with your entire client experience from client attraction strategies to how you deliver your programs and services and build long term relationships focused on value creation.

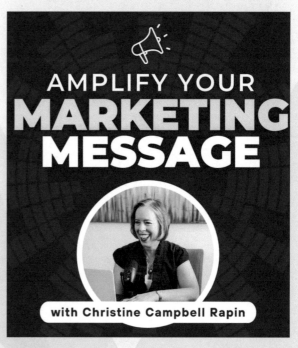

AMPLIFY YOUR
MARKETING MESSAGE

with Christine Campbell Rapin

BUSINESS SCALE ACCELERATOR
12 MONTH PROGRAM

1-1 Mentorship Program

Connect with Christine

Christine Campbell Rapin
Business Mentor & Consultant
+1-587-434-9944
Cochrane , Alberta
www.Christinecampbellrapin.com

Finally, remember that the first thing a buyer is investing in is the confidence you have in helping them achieve the results. If you lack confidence in either building or executing these 3 non-negotiables to attract clients consistently.

Business CAN be elegantly simple and requires effort.

Embrace these principles and you will create a client growth engine and finally stop struggling to build momentum in your business.

"MY MOM SAVED MY LIFE!"

ALEX DUMAS

These were the words of a client who worked with me for a half-day VIP experience. He told me that he never shared his story in that way before and forgot that detail as he explained a drug overdose that nearly ended his life.

As he described her experience, she heard a faint voice inside prompt her to check in on him during the night. She opened his door in horror to see him convulsing on his bed with foam pouring from his mouth. She panicked and screamed for her husband to help her.

His father was typically never home but for some reason, he was there that night and without him there, my client would have certainly passed away. They began CPR and called the ambulance where he was delivered to a local hospital.

Here's the thing: that near-death moment wasn't enough to scare him straight.
The grip of addiction was too strong and he continued using drugs for some time before finally making a powerful decision to get help and stay clean.

The story is inspiring but I'm sharing it with you to bring to life what he experienced when he practiced it with me.

He had never told it in that way before. He had never "acted" it out and he embodied the panic that his mother had at that moment.

He saw just how destructive his addiction was and that has propelled him to serve as many people in recovery as possible. My client experienced a breakthrough in delivering his story in a way that leaves a lasting impression on any stage he touches.

The men and women he sponsors can open up and feel safe without judgment because he knows exactly where they are on their sobriety journeys.

Can you relate?

How many times have you done something harmful, and were able to walk away yet you repeated the same behavior?

Have you been on a path of self-destruction and sworn to yourself "This is THE last time" only to come back?

What about your business? You know there's something you SHOULD be doing yet you sabotage yourself with distractions and activities that don't generate impact or income?

You don't have to have an extreme example like he had but there's gold in whatever you've experienced.

There's an amazing story of redemption and reflection that can benefit so many people in the world.

My invitation to you is this, would you like some help crafting and developing that story?

Would it benefit you to show up as a professional on podcasts, summits, conferences, and networking mixers with a clear, compelling, and unique story?

If your answer is Yes then my Brand Amplifier Experience is perfect for you.

Storytelling isn't just an art—it's the heartbeat of human connection and the secret weapon of wildly successful entrepreneurs. Here's why mastering your story is non-negotiable:

Instant Expert Status: Stories bypass their skepticism and position you as the go-to authority in your field.

Emotional Resonance: Stories forge deep, lasting connections with your audience that facts and figures can't touch.

Memorability Factor: Be the voice they remember long after the noise fades away.

Universal Language: Transcend cultural and professional barriers, speaking directly to the human experience.

Neurological Impact: Tap into the brain's hardwiring for narrative, making your message unforgettable.

I experienced these benefits directly when I revamped my online presence. I made a bold declaration by committing to expanding Black Excellence globally. This commitment has placed me on the path of ideal clients and invitations to contribute books and articles (like the one you're reading).

Here's how a powerful story and video helped me land a keynote. I recorded a podcast in a professional studio in Raleigh, NC in the Fall of 2023. When the episode was released, I shared it with many people within my network. I didn't have any intention of anything coming from that. If someone were to gain some valuable insights as a result, that would have been more than enough for me.

An Executive Director reached out to me shortly after watching it. He invited me to his company's annual conference which would be taking place in 3 weeks and I humbly accepted the invitation. They paid for my hotel, reimbursed my travel, and scheduled me to deliver the kickoff keynote.

I shared personal stories relating to my challenges with substance use as a teen and young adult. I connected with that audience and helped them gain a new perspective on how to communicate effectively and collaborate creatively.

Our words matter. They move people to action and the impact of a powerful story can extend far beyond your wildest dreams. What if I hadn't invested in myself to have new images and videos taken? What if I hadn't committed to hours of practice? Of re-writing my talk and having my peers offer feedback?

Just as my client realized, I saw for myself how valuable a well-crafted story and memorable delivery could shift others into inspired action.

Research shows that stories are 22 times more memorable than facts alone (Source: Jerome Bruner, cognitive psychologist)

Neural coupling increases by 75% when listening to stories, creating deep, lasting connections (Source: Princeton University)

Stories can boost conversion rates by up to 30% (Source: Stanford Graduate School of Business)

Throughout the 4-month Brand Amplifier Experience, you'll develop a powerhouse story that can translate on virtual and in-person platforms. You'll get surprise resources that will set you up for success as a speaker and thought leader. Last but not least, you'll have me in your corner, coaching you on and cheering for you to rise beyond your wildest dreams.

The field is where all of the fun is and when you play with me, YOU WIN! If you're ready to win big with your story, let's play. Learn More: *https://bit.ly/brand-amplifier*

Learn More About Alex At
www.alexdumascoaching.com
Learn More about the Brand Amplifier
Experience at **www.bit.ly/brand-amplifier**

Don't Make Silly Mistakes With Lifestyle Choices As It Affects Your Health and Well-being

Ngozi Chijioke-Agina

Ever wondered how daily habits impact health and well-being?

Imagine starting the day with a brisk walk, enjoying a balanced breakfast, and taking moments to breathe and relax. These small choices can make a huge difference in how someone feels, physically and mentally.

This blog post will explore how lifestyle choices affect health and well-being daily. It will dive into real-life stories and practical tips to help make healthier daily decisions.

Whether one is curious about

• maintaining a healthy body weight,
• lowering blood pressure,
• preventing cancer, or
• controlling type 2 diabetes, this post has something for them

By the end, it would be clear just how powerful choices can be.

Disclaimer: The information in this post is for educational purposes only and should not replace professional medical advice. A doctor should be consulted for personalized guidance.

What Are Healthy Lifestyle Choices?

Healthy lifestyle choices are decisions and daily habits contributing to overall health and happiness. These choices help people feel more energetic, reduce the risk of diseases, and improve mental well-being. They involve making mindful decisions that enhance the quality of life. Healthy lifestyle choices are sustainable habits that can be incorporated into daily routines. By prioritizing these choices, people can live longer, healthier lives filled with vitality and joy.

When I was younger, I used to think that good health was all about genetics and a sprinkle of luck. If someone was lucky, they'd stay healthy, and if not, well, tough luck, but then I witnessed my grandmother, who lived to be well over 100 years of age. She was full of life, always active, and never missed her daily chores until the very end. This made me realize that lifestyle choices affect health and well-being in ways I had never imagined.

Real-Life Success Stories

Case Study #1:

A friend was diagnosed with breast cancer. It was a difficult time for her family, but her doctor gave them hope that lifestyle changes may help reverse it. Cancer is a scary word, but there are ways to reduce the risk. The lifestyle changes to prevent cancer are within control. Avoiding tobacco, limiting alcohol, eating plenty of fruits and vegetables, and staying active can lower the chances. It's empowering to know that choices can protect people.

Case Study #2:

Lisa used to struggle with her body weight for years. She tried every diet she could find, but nothing seemed to work. She used to get headaches a lot too, and was told that her blood pressure was a bit high. Then, after the diagnosis, she started making small lifestyle changes: choosing fruits over chips, walking instead of taking the bus, and drinking water instead of soda. It wasn't an overnight transformation, but gradually, she saw the numbers on the scale go down. It's amazing how lifestyle choices impact weight management!

To everyone's surprise, her headaches disappeared, and she felt more energetic. It turns out that lifestyle changes can lower blood pressure significantly as well. It's not just about taking pills; it's about making smart, healthy choices every single day.

Case Study #3:

Then there's my cousin, Glo, who had type 2 diabetes a few years ago. At first, it seemed like the end of the world for her. However, her doctor encouraged her to make some necessary lifestyle changes. She started watching what she ate, exercising as much as she could, at her age {she was over 60 years then}, and monitoring her blood sugar levels. It wasn't easy, but she managed to get her diabetes under control. Seeing Glo's journey taught me how powerful lifestyle choices for type 2 diabetes can be. It's about making consistent, healthy choices that become part of a daily routine.

I decided to take a closer look at how daily habits can change lives. From what people eat, and how much they exercise, to how they manage stress—and found out that every little choice matters.

So, what can be done so more people benefit?

Transforming Health with Simple Choices
Here are some aspects of healthy lifestyle choices:

[1] A Balanced Diet:
Eating or filling a plate with colorful fruits and vegetables, whole grains, lean proteins, and healthy fats. Limiting sugary drinks, processed foods, and high-fat snacks. Staying hydrated by drinking plenty of water.

[2] Regular Exercise:
Ensuring at least 30 minutes of moderate physical activity most days of the week. A mix of cardio, strength training, and flexibility exercises will do. Finding enjoyable activities, like walking, cycling, swimming, or dancing.

[3] Mental Wellbeing:
Managing stress through activities like meditation, or deep-breathing exercises. Trying to get enough sleep (at least 7-9 hours per night). Seeking social connections and support from friends and family.

[4] Preventive Healthcare:
Going for regular check-ups and screenings to catch potential health issues early. Staying up-to-date with vaccinations.
Avoiding as much as possible habits like smoking and excessive alcohol consumption.

[5] Healthy Habits:
Maintaining a healthy weight through balanced eating and regular activity. Practicing good hygiene and self-care routines.

Setting realistic goals and tracking progress towards a healthier lifestyle.

By making these healthy lifestyle choices, there is an improved energy levels, mood, and overall health, which lead to a longer, happier life.

Consider this for a moment...

What small changes can be made today? Maybe walking to the store instead of driving or choosing a salad over a burger.
Each choice is a step towards a healthier body.

It is fascinating how daily habits shape someone's future. Just like my grandmother, everyone has the power to live long, healthy lives by making wise lifestyle choices. Whether it's maintaining a healthy body weight, lowering blood pressure, preventing cancer, or controlling diabetes, every little change counts.

So, why not start today?

It takes that first step, to make a small change, for a glorious future that will thank you.

And who knows?

It might inspire others to do the same, just like Lisa, my Grandmother, and Glo inspired me.

The Journey to Better Health Starts Now

These changes don't have to be automatic, starting small by swapping out one unhealthy habit for a healthy one, is recommended. Over time, these small changes add up to bring transformation.

CHANGE FOR GOOD

By Heidi Johnson

hange is the one constant in life we all share. How funny we are that we fight the one thing we know to be true? Change is all around us. As humans we love change once it has happened but we typically fear and hate the idea of anything changing that is ahead of us. And yet, we all go in search of help to change. We want to be richer, thinner, happier and we want a self help book to show us the way.

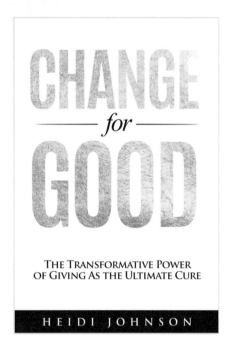

CHANGE *for* **GOOD**

THE TRANSFORMATIVE POWER OF GIVING AS THE ULTIMATE CURE

H E I D I   J O H N S O N

There are over 15,000 self help books published each year. Currently, the self help market is estimated to be around eleven billion dollars. There is no end in sight to this self help craze ending with the industry predicting to expand to over fifteen billion dollars in 2025. In full disclosure, I love self help books and have read more than my fair share of them.

What is great about self help books is that they refocus our attention in a very noisy world. If we want to improve our finances, we read money managing books. The chances are high that our energy will follow our attention. As a result, we focus on our money habits and they will improve. This is why we read these books and why they work.

It is also why I decided to write one. I think we are focusing on the wrong things to improve. Why are we not looking to change for good? When our one short precious life comes to an end is anyone going to talk about your weight or your bank account at your funeral? No! They are going to talk about how you made people feel, who you helped and how you made the world better. This is what we should all be focusing on because this is what really matters. There is no silver bullet for life. All of us get dealt a bad hand or two. The question is how do we play that bad hand? Or another way to look at it is what do we do with that pain? How do we use it for purpose?

The question is much simpler than the answer. The short answer is it is a process. Think of your bad hand (a divorce, a death, a job loss, a move, etc) as a trash can.

MONTHLY COLUMNIST

Whatever happened is your trash. You can let the trash sit there and rot within you or you can decide to recycle. Bad energy can be turned into good but it takes time. That change is a slow process.

As someone who took pain from a tragic accident and turned it into a nonprofit, I understand. When tragedy struck, all I knew was that my beautiful life was in shambles. What I learned was that really living begins with loss. There is no forest without a fire. Without an earthquake, there is no new city. Loss hits us like a landslide and it all just comes down and we are buried not sure which way is up. Little by little, we begin to dig. And with each shovel towards the light, we become stronger in our belief that we will get out from under.

After digging my way out and using my pain for good, I wanted to find who were the other people who used their pain to help others? I went in search of the 1.6 million nonprofit founders in the United States. Wanting to know what was their story? For the past thirteen years, I have been learning from these incredible humans by interviewing them for the Charity Matters Blog and Podcast. The book, Change for Good, is not only my journey in healing through service but theirs as well.

My hope is that this new self help book will inspire people to use their pain for good. When we lean into our communities, we become more connected and joyful. Our resilience and strength come from overcoming the challenges. Our lives can radically shift for the better once we come through the other side.

This is how we begin to change for good.

Connect With Heidi

www.charity-matters.com

Now Available

BEYOND THE SMILE

A testament to the universal truth that behind every smile lies a story of triumphs and tribulations

SCAN TO ORDER

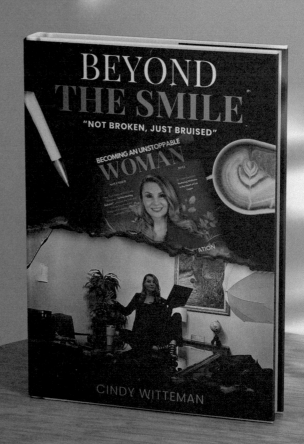

Finding Your Voice: A Business Mom's Journey to Visibility and Success

Nina Macarie

Have you ever felt like you don't have a voice in your business? As an introvert and self-described shy kid, I never imagined becoming a visibility expert and podcast manager for online business moms. If you've ever believed that not knowing everything about a topic disqualifies you from speaking about it, you're not alone. This mindset, combined with the challenges of returning to work after being a stay-at-home mom, can leave you feeling lost and unsure of your next steps.

Maybe you've found yourself in a similar situation: "After being a SAHM for more than 5 years - my personal choice - I found myself lost, not knowing who I was, what I liked, or what I wanted to do next. I had big plans before having kids, but they didn't make sense anymore." This feeling of being at a crossroads is common for many moms transitioning back into the professional world, especially when considering entrepreneurship.

Your breakthrough might come, as mine did, when you realize you can use your skills to support others in a similar position. This realization can lead you to start your own venture, even if you have initial self-doubts. Think about it: there are other moms out there, a little bit further along in their entrepreneurial journey, who might be looking for support from someone just like you. Your experiences, both as a mom and as a professional, give you a unique perspective that can be incredibly valuable to others.

Don't let a lack of fame hold you back. You don't need to be world-famous to make an impact – you just need to be in the right rooms and connect with the right people. Remember, people become interested in what you have to say when you give them a reason to care. That's why relationships matter so much in business. Each connection you make, each conversation you have, can open doors to new opportunities and collaborations.

Feeling overwhelmed by the prospect of putting yourself out there? It's a common concern, but there are ways to ease into it. Start small. You don't need a big email list to begin. There are ways to get interviewed on podcasts or summits or be part of bundles where an email list isn't the main requirement. This approach allows you to gain visibility and refine your message without the pressure of a large following. Each small step builds your confidence and helps you clarify your message.

Here's a practical and doable process for gaining visibility:
1. Identify your strengths and expertise: Reflect on your skills and experiences. What unique perspective can you offer? Your journey as a mom and professional has given you insights that others might find valuable.

2. Start with small steps: Join podcasts, participate in online summits or bundles, or attend virtual networking events. Each small action builds momentum. Don't underestimate the power of these seemingly minor actions – they can lead to significant opportunities.

3. Refine your message through repeated exposure: The more you speak about your topic, the clearer and more impactful your message becomes. Pay attention to which parts of your story resonate most with your audience and build on those.

4. Build relationships within your industry: Focus on genuine connections rather than transactional networking. Authentic relationships not only lead to business opportunities but also provide support and encouragement along your entrepreneurial journey.

5. Continuously invest in skill-building: Never stop learning and improving your craft. The business world is constantly evolving, and staying current keeps you relevant and confident.

Remember, confidence isn't a prerequisite for success – it's a byproduct of taking action and persevering. Each time you push past your comfort zone, you're building the confidence that will carry you forward in your business.

As you grow your business, keep in mind that it's not just about reaching your destination. It's also about what happens on your way there. Value the learning process as much as the end goal. Every challenge you overcome and every skill you acquire contributes to your personal and professional growth. These experiences shape you as an entrepreneur and as a person, making your journey unique and valuable.

Balancing business growth with family life is challenging, and it's okay to acknowledge that. "I remember the evenings where I'd tell my husband I only needed to send one email, and that would turn into hours of work," Nina recalls. While passion and dedication fuel your entrepreneurial journey, be careful not to fall into the trap of feeling you must do everything in your business at once. Don't lose sight of work-life balance by trying to apply every strategy that works for someone else. It's crucial to find a rhythm that works for you and your family.

Finding the right support system is crucial to keep your business going and maintain your motivation during difficult moments. Your spouse might not fully understand the challenges of working on your business, taking care of the household, and managing the kids' schedules all at once. This is where seeking out a community of like-minded business moms becomes invaluable for growth and support. These connections can provide understanding, advice, and encouragement that family members, despite their best intentions, might not be able to offer.

As you grow, you'll likely witness your own transformation. You might find yourself securing TV appearances, delivering TEDx talks, or hosting in-person events. These successes aren't just about business growth – they represent personal transformations and the realization of long-held dreams. Each milestone, no matter how small it might seem, is a testament to your growth and perseverance.

Remember, entrepreneurial success isn't about changing who you are or faking confidence. It's about embracing your authentic self and consistently showing up for your business and your clients. You don't need to be someone else; you just need to show more of who you are. Let this authenticity become the cornerstone of your approach to visibility and business growth. Your unique experiences and perspective are what will set you apart in a crowded market.

If you're struggling with visibility, remember: You have a voice, and you can find it. Whether you take baby steps or a big leap, be willing to try, test, and repeat. Challenge yourself to do things you're afraid of, while also being patient with your own growth process. Every successful entrepreneur has faced moments of doubt and fear – what sets them apart is their willingness to push through these challenges.

For introverts, podcasting can be a great visibility tool. It allows you to showcase your expertise and build connections without the pressure of live video or in-person networking. You can prepare your thoughts in advance, speak from the comfort of your own space, and still reach a wide audience. This medium can be a powerful way to share your message and connect with your ideal clients.

Your journey to finding your voice and growing your business won't always be linear. Expect setbacks and moments of doubt, but celebrate each step forward as a victory. "Little by little, I made progress by taking small steps. Sometimes two forward and three back, but I kept going," is a mantra worth adopting. Resilience and persistence are key traits of successful entrepreneurs – cultivate these in yourself.

As you navigate your business journey, remember that your experiences as a mom give you unique insights and skills. Time management, multitasking, patience, and problem-solving are all skills you've honed through parenting. These translate powerfully into the business world, giving you an edge that you might not even realize you have.

If you're looking to take the next step in gaining visibility and growing your online presence, connect with Nina on Instagram **(https://instagram.com/nina_macarie)** and reach out if you're struggling with visibility in your business. Don't underestimate the power of reaching out and asking for help or guidance – it's a strength, not a weakness.

Remember, every big success starts with a small step. With persistence, authenticity, and the right support, you can find your voice and use it to create the business and life you dream of. The path may not always be easy, but it's undoubtedly worth it. Your unique voice and perspective are needed in the world – don't be afraid to let them shine. By showing up authentically and consistently, you're not just building a business – you're inspiring others and creating a ripple effect of empowerment among business moms. Your voice has the power to change lives – including your own. So, take that first step, or that next step, with confidence. The world is waiting to hear what you have to say.

Why Businesses Have a Responsibility to Give Back

By Liz Toombs

Giving back to the community has not only inspired Liz Toombs, a renowned Certified Interior Decorator, but brought her immense personal satisfaction over the last 15 years as both an entrepreneur and owner of the firm PDR Interiors. It was a mindset first instilled as a little girl growing up in Louisville and later solidified during her time as an undergraduate and member of the sorority Alpha Gamma Delta at the University of Kentucky.

She believes giving back is an inherent responsibility and integral part of creating not only a positive work environment but boosting employee morale for every business regardless of size. This can take many different forms, and you could team up with other colleagues or go on your own. It could be serving the hungry at a soup kitchen, visiting with the residents of an assisted living community, or giving comfort to cats and dogs at an animal shelter. It could be sponsoring a charity event or providing pro bono services in support of a specific philanthropic initiative.

Liz understands the degree and level to which one can give back depends on many factors and that giving back may not necessarily take the most obvious form of treasure or financial resources. Giving back can also include the contribution of time or talent through one's professional skill set or expertise. What you can give back in terms of time and talent is largely dictated by your schedule and other duties be they job-related or at home. And your calendar may be such that you can only give on average an hour a week – perhaps even less - due to various constraints. It's also important to note that with the flexibility in work schedules offered by many employers today, you aren't solely limited to the window of volunteering just on the weekends or on weeknights.

When choosing one or more organizations to support, Liz believes it is imperative you are passionate about that group's mission, understand the market it serves, and how impactful it is delivering results to its target audience. Perhaps you can get behind a cause because it has direct relevance in your own life. You provided a home for an animal rescue or you had a loved one battle and unfortunately succumb to a specific disease. If you need to find a charity and want to check on its credentials, if it aligns with your values and how much money they actually give back to the organization's mission, there are many ways to do that, including using a highly reputable resource called Charity Navigator.

It is Liz's hands-on involvement with multiple nonprofit organizations she has found enormously rewarding. The Junior League - an educational women's volunteer organization aimed at improving communities and the social, cultural, and political fabric of civil society – has 295 chapters and for the last 14 years she has been closely associated with the chapter in Lexington, Kentucky. Many of the nonprofit organizations she served during her professional life is a result of her involvement with The Junior League.

Liz has also been involved with the American Cancer Society, chairing several of their events including Denim & Diamonds as well as Belles and Beaus. It was the ultimate honor when she was recognized as a cancer survivor at the Society's Purse, Pouts and Pearls fundraiser in 2016. She made a full recovery after being diagnosed with melanoma in 2008.

The Mary Estes Memorial Scholarship Liz launched at the University of Kentucky – in honor of Liz's mother who passed away from cancer in 2012 - supports students who have also lost a parent to cancer. To date, five students have benefited from the scholarship, a few of whom even received funding support in consecutive years during their undergraduate careers.

You don't need to feel the pressure to start a scholarship, chair a fundraising event, or volunteer with one organization for 14 years. All you need is a basic willingness and desire to help and then take the first step by reaching out to a group that has captured your attention. They will be thrilled to have your interest and will tell you exactly how you can get involved!

Mentoring college-age and young professional women is another way Liz has given back. It was first at the University of Kentucky where she learned the value of having a mentor. Then as a young professional, she encountered a stable of amazing women that were worthy of emulation. One of the most special was a client Liz worked with for more than a decade. She had a penchant for mentoring and fostering young talent throughout her life. She came to her with wild ideas for her home and had full confidence that she would figure out how to make them come to fruition. Her belief in Liz gave her the confidence to try new things and explore design options she would not have considered otherwise.

Very few of the moments shared over the years with women Liz has mentored were formal appointments with a goal to discuss a certain topic or for her to learn a new life skill. Most of these moments just happened and she didn't recognize how much they shaped her until many years later. Mentorship is rarely an official arrangement, and it can't be forced. Instead, it is a relationship fostered naturally where one woman teaches, encourages, or shares her life experiences with another. Liz recognized how the mentors who supported her gave her the confidence to get to the next stage of her life. When she examines how she approaches relationships in her life, she sees the reflection of these special women. This is why mentoring is a keystone of her firm today.

Liz is contacted by countless students and young professionals about breaking into the design field. She never turns down any request for a meeting. At the very least she takes a coffee meeting. Do you know what happens every time? The conversation gives her a sense of purpose. When she talks about her career path, she is reminded that all the experiences she has had happened for a reason. Even if that reason is only to share it with someone else to help them as they navigate a similar situation.

Giving back should not be viewed as a chore. It should be something you want to do. And if you don't feel your heart is into it, switch gears. The last thing an organization wants is a volunteer who doesn't want to be there and isn't present. Nonprofits have enough obstacles and challenges to face.

Liz's ultimate hope is that you will find something you like to do to outside the office in terms of giving back that enriches your life the way her experiences have enriched her life. She is forever grateful for those many opportunities to grow both as a professional and as a human being.

Connect With Liz

🌐 pdr-interiors.com

📷 www.instagram.com/pdrinteriors

♪ www.tiktok.com/@pdr_interiors

Empowering Social Entrepreneurs: The Journey to Fulfillment and Impact

By Wayne Veldsman

In the ever-changing world of social entrepreneurship, the path to success is often paved with challenges, setbacks, and moments of self-doubt. Yet, it is these obstacles that develop the resilient spirit of a true changemaker.

Throughout this article, we will take a look into how fulfillment and empowerment are connected, and we'll find out how communication, emotional intelligence, and leadership, transform not only your business but also your life's journey.

Finding Your Sweet Spot in Entrepreneurship

Now, let's talk about fulfillment. It's not just about watching those dollars roll in (though that's nice too!). It's about waking up every day, pumped to make a difference.

Growing up as a first-generation immigrant in a not-so-well-off household, I've faced my fair share of hurdles. But you know what? Those challenges shaped how I see the world today.

Here's the secret sauce: true fulfillment comes from mashing together what you love with making a positive impact. It's about creating a ripple effect that leaves the world a bit better than you found it.

So, for all you social entrepreneurs out there, here's your mission:
Figure out what makes you tick and align your business with it.
Regularly check in: are you actually making a difference for your target community?
Celebrate those wins, no matter how small! Progress is progress, folks!

Supercharging Your Impact

Alright, let's talk empowerment. At its core? Communication. And I'm not just talking about chatting with others!
Here's the thing: empowerment isn't about having all the answers or always making the right call. It's about asking meaningful questions, really actively listening (not just waiting for your turn to talk), and keeping moving forward based on what you learn. Master these skills, and you'll be building relationships like a pro and empowering yourself to reach new heights!

Here are three steps to further empower yourself and others through communication:

- *When someone's talking, really listen! Be genuinely curious, listen closely, rephrase back what you hear to ensure you're on the same page, and don't be focused on what you're going to say next.*
- *Ask questions that make people think; questions that don't just get a yes or no answer.*
- *Try to see things from the other person's perspective. Walk a mile in their shoes; be empathetic!*

Your Entrepreneurial Superpower: Resilience

Let me tell you, entrepreneurship is one heck of a rollercoaster. Since I started my first business back in 2013, I've had more setbacks than I can count. And I bet if you're reading this, you've had your fair share too.

Want to hear some of my greatest hits?

- *I battled clinical anxiety and depression for over 10 years.*
- *At 21, I fell off a roof, nearly lost my life, and woke up not knowing if I was paralyzed.*
- *One month after being hired for my first marketing job, I got blindsided and unfairly fired.*

In 2017 we launched a QR code focused restaurant menu's company... only to give up 15 months before COVID hit... (Facepalm moment, right?)
In our world, challenges and setbacks are like our daily bread. I've started eight different companies before founding JourneyToLegacy.org, and less than half turned a profit. But guess what? We keep pushing forward.
So, how do you build that resilient, "delusion optimism" muscle?
Reframe those failures. They're not failures, they're learning opportunities!
Cultivate a growth mindset. Embrace those challenges! You can change!
Build your support squad! Find fellow entrepreneurs and mentors who get it.

The Secret Sauce of Leadership: Emotional Intelligence

Alright, social entrepreneurs, listen up as this is a big one! Your emotional intelligence (EQ) can make or break your success. But what the heck is EQ? It's all about understanding and managing your own emotions while also tuning into others'.

Want to boost your EQ? Focus on these three areas:

- *Self-awareness: Get to know yourself. Your emotions, strengths, weaknesses, and how you impact others.*

- *Empathy: Try to really understand where others are coming from. Validate their feelings and show some compassion.*

- *Active Listening: Really hear what people are saying. Don't just wait for your turn to talk. Get curious, nod, make eye contact, show them you're engaged.*

Alright, so up until now we've talked a big game about fulfillment and empowerment. But how do we actually make it happen for the long run? In our Journey To Legacy Community, we've boiled it down to three key areas. Don't worry, it's not rocket science – just simple, everyday stuff that can make a big difference.

1. Daily Habits: Your Secret Weapon

First up, let's chat about daily habits. These are your bread and butter, folks. Every day, work to grow in three main areas: your mental health, your physical health, and your financial health. It might sound like a lot, but trust me, if you can nail these three, you'll be ready to tackle just about anything life throws at you.

2. Networking & Support

I get it – in this world of remote work and Zoom calls, it can feel pretty lonely sometimes. Especially in our industry! That's why connecting with others is so crucial. Find your tribe – people who get you, who share your passions. That's exactly why we started the Journey To Legacy Community. We're all about bringing together folks who want to make a difference. So come join us – we're on a mission to leave this world a little better than we found it.

3. Mindfulness: It's Not Just for Yogis (Mental Health)

Last but definitely not least, let's talk about mindfulness. Now, before you roll your eyes, hear me out. This isn't about sitting cross-legged on a mountain top. It's simply about learning to control your thoughts instead of letting them control you. Start small – even just a few minutes a day can make a difference. Use an app like Calm or Insight Timer if you need some guidance, and don't get discouraged your first time; stick with it, and you'll be amazed at how it can help you manage stress and stay focused.

Remember, it's all about taking small steps every day. You don't have to change your whole life overnight. Just focus on these areas bit by bit, and before you know it, you'll be well on your way to a more fulfilling, empowering journey.

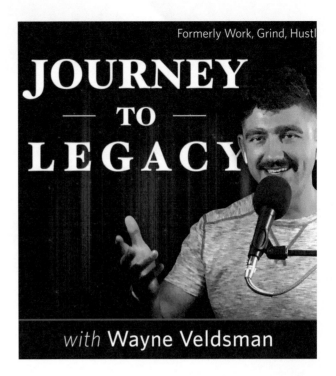

Wrapping It Up

So there you have it, fellow change-makers! The path of a social entrepreneur is never smooth sailing, but it is rewarding! By focusing on fulfillment, empowerment, communication, and emotional intelligence, you're not just setting yourself up for business success – you're gearing up to make a real difference!

Remember, through positivity, patience, and never stopping learning, we can achieve anything.

Ready to take this seriously? Come join us in the Journey To Legacy Community at *journeytolegacy.org.* Connect with other awesome folks who are all about personal growth and making an impact.

Your journey to creating a lasting legacy starts right now. Embrace those challenges, celebrate every win (no matter how small), and never stop believing in your power to make a difference.

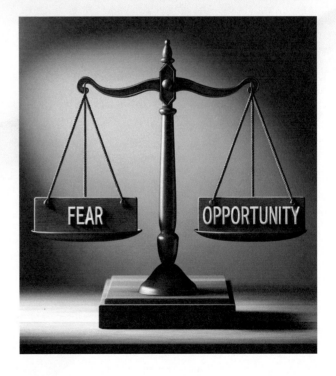

HOW TO MONETIZE YOUR INFLUENCE IN Q4: A FOCUS ON DECISION-MAKING, CLOSING, PROSPECTING STRATEGIES, AND OPTIMIZATION

By Bridget Hom

As the year enters its final stretch, entrepreneurs and influencers find themselves at a pivotal moment. The fourth quarter, often seen as the last big push to hit revenue goals, is where success is determined by those who make bold moves and execute with precision. Monetizing your influence in Q4 means focusing on key elements: decision-making, closing, prospecting strategies, and optimization. Each of these areas requires thoughtful action to convert influence into tangible results. Remember, taking imperfect action leads to massive results.

1. Decision-Making: The Foundation of Success

In Q4, decisions need to be swift, intentional, and based on clear objectives. "What is the goal" is a phrase to memorize. Entrepreneurs who are waiting for the "perfect" moment to act or feel overwhelmed by too many options may find themselves missing out on opportunities. Successful decision-making is about clarity—knowing where you want to go and what steps will get you there.

The first step in effective decision-making is to look at the data. What has worked well throughout the year? Which strategies haven't yielded the expected results? In Q4, there's no time for guesswork. Decisions should be based on performance metrics and informed by the lessons learned in previous quarters.

Once you have clarity, it's time to make bold moves. Whether it's launching a new product, ramping up marketing efforts, or pivoting strategies entirely, entrepreneurs must take full ownership of every decision they make. There's no room for hesitation. Ownership breeds action, and action breeds results. The businesses that thrive in Q4 are the ones that make informed, intentional decisions and follow through with unwavering commitment to empower more people with their incredible solutions!

2. Closing: Master the Art of Sealing the Deal

December is the biggest buying month of the year. Once decisions have been made, the focus shifts to closing. Closing sales is the lifeblood of any Q4 monetization strategy, and it requires a refined approach. During the final months of the year, consumers are ready to make purchases—whether it's for holiday shopping, end-of-year business investments, or preparing for the next year's goals. This makes it the perfect time for entrepreneurs to push for high-conversion offers that solve immediate problems for their audience.

Closing effectively requires confidence and clarity in communication. Here's where the groundwork laid throughout the year pays off. The trust built through content, social proof, and consistent engagement needs to be leveraged to close sales quickly and efficiently. When entrepreneurs present offers, it should be with a sense of urgency, limited-time benefits, and clear calls to action that inspire immediate decisions from prospects.

Moreover, overcoming objections is key. In Q4, potential clients may hesitate due to budget concerns or fear of making the wrong decision before year-end. This is the time to address those concerns head-on, offering solutions such as flexible payment options, special bonuses, or guarantees that eliminate risk. Great closers don't just sell; they reassure, inspire confidence, and make it easy for prospects to say "yes" without hesitation.

3. Prospecting Strategies: Powerful Prospecting requires imperfect action

In Q4, entrepreneurs need to take imperfect action about prospecting. The time to build relationships with potential clients is running out, and those who succeed will be the ones who approach prospecting with a strategic, results-driven mindset.

The goal is simple: maximize your reach and engagement by tapping into your existing network while also identifying new people to empower with your solution. The first step is to leverage your influence—whether through social media, email campaigns, or webinars. By positioning yourself as the go-to expert in your field, you create demand and attract new prospects who are eager for solutions.

Here are three prospecting strategies that work well in Q4:

- Webinars and Masterclasses: Offering a high-value, low-cost (or even free) webinar is an excellent way to pull prospects into your funnel. By sharing expertise, addressing pain points, and offering solutions, you can quickly establish authority and convert attendees into paying clients.

- LinkedIn Outreach: In Q4, many businesses are looking to make final investments in services or products that can boost their Q1 outcomes. LinkedIn is a powerful platform for identifying and engaging with decision-makers. A targeted outreach campaign—sending personalized connection requests and offering value-driven insights—can fill your pipeline with high-quality leads.

- Referral Programs: Turn your existing customers into brand ambassadors by offering referral incentives. Satisfied clients who've benefited from your services are more likely to recommend you to others in their network. A strong referral program can help you acquire new clients quickly, with minimal effort.

4. Optimization: Maximize Efficiency and Results

To truly dominate in Q4, businesses need to focus on optimization. Every element of their sales and marketing strategy should be fine-tuned to ensure maximum efficiency and effectiveness. There's no time to waste on strategies that don't deliver results. Instead, entrepreneurs should focus on scaling what works and eliminating what doesn't.

Here's how to optimize key areas for Q4:

- Sales Funnels: Review your existing sales funnels. Are they converting as expected? If not, where are prospects dropping off? Simple tweaks like improving email subject lines, refining CTAs (calls to action), or offering more attractive upsells can significantly increase conversions. The goal is to optimize your funnel for maximum revenue per lead.

- Content Strategy: In Q4, your content should be laser-focused on the needs of your audience. Now is not the time to be overly broad or generic. Speak directly to the urgent problems your clients are facing and offer solutions that align with their year-end goals. High-impact content—like case studies, testimonials, and solution-oriented posts—will help push prospects to take action.

- Empowering Client Interactions: Happy clients mean repeat business and referrals. Optimize the client experience by going above and beyond. Whether it's through exceptional customer service, follow-up emails, or offering unexpected bonuses, ensuring that clients feel valued will encourage long-term loyalty and increased revenue.

- Task Management and Mind Management: Q4 is fast-paced, and time is a precious resource. Streamlining operations—whether it's automating administrative tasks, delegating responsibilities, or using productivity tools—frees up more time to focus on high-priority activities like closing sales and nurturing leads and stay empowering in your conversations! Remember, your prospects will remember how you make them feel. Doing intentional mindset work in the morning will prepare the entrepreneur for being productive, proactive, and profitable!

Conclusion: Finish Strong by Owning Your Q4 Strategy

The entrepreneurs who take ownership of their decisions, execute a strong closing strategy, adopt proactive prospecting tactics, and optimize their processes will be the ones who finish Q4 with success. In the world of business, influence is not enough—it must be combined with decisive action, a strategic focus, and a commitment to maximizing results.

By making bold decisions, mastering the art of closing, prospecting like a pro, and optimizing every area of your business, you can transform your influence into measurable revenue and close out the year on top. The time to act is now—Q4 is your final stage to leverage all the hard work you've put in throughout the year. Seize it, and own the success that awaits.

Connect with Bridget

www.bridgetofreedomcoaching.com

Schedule your free 30 minute direction session today!

www.bridgethom.me

HOW TO STAY FOCUSED IN A SALES OR ENTREPRENEURIAL ROLE:
A GUIDE FOR WOMEN IN BUSINESS

By Samantha Sheppard

In the fast-paced world of sales and entrepreneurship, staying focused can feel like an uphill battle. With multiple tasks, clients, and projects all demanding your attention, it's easy to get overwhelmed. But what if there was a way to streamline your focus, boost your productivity, and achieve success without burning out?

In this article, we'll explore three powerful strategies to help you stay focused: 90-minute sprints, creating your ideal work environment, and the power of small, consistent actions.

The Power of 90-Minute Sprints (Batching)

One of the most effective productivity techniques for busy women in business is the 90-minute sprint. This method involves focusing intensely on a single task or batching similar tasks together for 90 minutes, followed by a 15-minute break. But why 90 minutes? Research suggests that our brains can only maintain intense focus for about 90 minutes before needing a break. By working within this natural rhythm, you can maximize your productivity without exhausting yourself.

Why 90-Minute Sprints Work:
- **Aligns with Natural Attention Spans**: The human brain is wired to focus best in short bursts. A 90-minute sprint allows you to work at your peak performance, after which a break helps you recharge and prepare for the next task.
- **Reduces Mental Fatigue**: By focusing on one task or similar tasks, you minimize the mental energy required to switch between different activities, which can be draining and inefficient.

How to Implement 90-Minute Sprints:
- **Start with Prioritization**: Begin your day by identifying the most critical tasks. Decide which tasks can be grouped together and set a timer for 90 minutes to focus solely on those tasks.
- **Take Breaks Seriously**: After each 90-minute sprint, take a 15-minute break. Use this time to stretch, grab a healthy snack, refill your coffee cup or simply relax. This helps to refresh your mind and keeps you energized throughout the day.
- **Batch Similar Tasks**: For instance, you could dedicate one sprint to lead generation, another to client follow-ups, and another to content creation. Batching similar tasks minimizes the mental load of switching between different activities, allowing you to dive deeper into each task.

Setting Up Your Ideal Work Environment

Your environment plays a crucial role in your ability to stay focused. If your workspace isn't working for you, it's working against you. A well-designed workspace not only boosts your productivity but also inspires creativity and motivation.

Why Your Work Environment Matters:
- Minimizes Distractions: A cluttered or chaotic workspace can lead to distractions, making it difficult to maintain focus on the task at hand.

MONTHLY COLUMNIST

- **Enhances Comfort and Efficiency**: An ergonomic setup and a well-organized space contribute to comfort and efficiency, reducing the physical and mental strain that can come from working in a less-than-ideal environment.
- **Boosts Mood and Motivation**: A workspace that reflects your personality and goals can inspire you and keep you motivated throughout the day.

Tips for Creating Your Ideal Workspace:
- **Declutter**: Start by removing any unnecessary items from your workspace. A clean and organized desk can do wonders for your focus.
- **Ensure Comfort**: Invest in a comfortable chair, and make sure your desk is at the right height. Ergonomic comfort is key to maintaining focus over long periods.
- **Optimize Lighting**: Natural light is best, but if that's not an option, ensure your workspace is well-lit with warm, bright lighting that keeps you alert.
- **Add Personal Touches**: Surround yourself with things that inspire you, whether it's a vision board, motivational quotes, or photos of loved ones. These personal touches can make your workspace more enjoyable and motivating.
- **Action Step**: Take a few minutes to assess your current workspace. Identify any changes you can make to reduce distractions and enhance comfort. Even small adjustments can have a significant impact on your focus and productivity.

The Power of Small Disciplines Repeated Over Time

In the pursuit of big goals, it's easy to overlook the power of small, consistent actions. However, the key to achieving significant success often lies in the daily disciplines we commit to. These small actions, when repeated consistently over time, can lead to massive results.

Why Small Disciplines Matter:
- **Compound Effect**: Small actions might seem insignificant in the short term, but over time, they compound and create significant outcomes.
- **Builds Momentum**: Consistently completing small tasks builds momentum, making it easier to tackle larger challenges and achieve your goals.
- **Reduces Overwhelm**: Focusing on small, manageable tasks prevents the overwhelm that can come from trying to do everything at once.

Examples of Small Disciplines:
- Daily Follow-Ups: Committing to a set number of follow-up calls each day can gradually build a strong client base and improve sales.
- Personal Development: Dedicating just 15 minutes a day to reading or learning something new can significantly enhance your skills and knowledge over time.
- Content Creation: Posting consistently on social media, even if it's just once a day, can increase your online presence and engagement.

It's easy to get caught up in the big picture and forget that success is built one step at a time. Focus on the small, daily disciplines that will move you closer to your goals. Remember, it's the consistent effort that leads to long-term success.

- Action Step: Identify one small discipline you can commit to every day. It could be as simple as setting aside 10 minutes to plan your day or sending a quick thank-you note to a client. Whatever it is, make it a habit and watch how it transforms your business over time.

Connect with Samantha
www.samanthasheppardconsulting.com

Staying focused in a sales or entrepreneurial role is no small feat, but with the right strategies, you can boost your productivity and achieve your goals without burning out. By implementing 90-minute sprints, creating an ideal work environment, and committing to small, consistent actions, you'll set yourself up for long-term success.

Remember, focus isn't about doing more; it's about doing what matters most with intention and clarity. So, take these strategies and start applying them to your daily routine. You'll be amazed at the difference they can make in your productivity and overall business success!

My Lazarus Experience: How God Saved My Life

By Catherine Garrett

As we entered 2019 my sweet little family could never have imagined the coming storm. Even though we didn't know what was to come, God did. As hard as it was and still is, that helps me find comfort.

Early in the morning on September 18, 2019, I awoke to having mild contractions around 2 am. Fast forward about 10 hours my husband and I would walk into the hospital to deliver our daughter. This would be the last time I would breathe fresh air for 24 days.

About 22 hours later I would go into cardiopulmonary arrest for the first time. Over the next several hours, I would arrest a total of 6 times. In the story of Lazarus, he was dead for multiple days and Jesus raised him from the dead. Similar to Lazarus and his loved ones, we would need to submit to the Lord's plan and trust.

While in labor with my second daughter, we would experience an amniotic fluid embolism. It is thought to be the result of an allergic-like reaction to amniotic fluid that enters the mother's bloodstream; a normal part of the birth process.

My daughter would need to be resuscitated and rushed to the NICU. Miraculously, she recovered incredibly well and was in the NICU for less than a week.

Unfortunately, my recovery has been much longer.

What would occur over the next 9 days is nothing short of a herculean feat.
Hundreds of medical heroes.
7 surgeries.
5 days on Extracorporeal Membrane Oxygenation.
A stroke.
And tens of thousands of people around the world, praying for our family.

Now knowing the stats of what our family went through, I think we have a pretty good assertion of how to weather hard seasons. Given enough time, everyone will go through a "hurricane" of some sort. If I may, allow me to encourage you!

First, hold faith. I would argue, that there isn't much that is harder than walking into a hospital to have a baby and being wheeled out disabled. We never stopped praying and held faith that everything would be ok; even if the outcome is not what we would have picked. Now, I know everyone is not religious, but this still applies. Whether you are religious or not holding hope is still important. Mindset is key.

Second, write out a training plan. You are probably asking yourself "A training plan? What is that?!" I am a former animal trainer. Anytime you want to teach an animal a new behavior the first step is always to write down the goals and work out a training plan. One example in my recovery is driving. I couldn't just get in a car and drive. Did you know, there are about 10-20 different things a person is doing all at once when they are driving? I had to relearn how to do all of these.

Third, expect setbacks. If you have spent any amount of time with anyone in recovery (whether physical or mental), you know the saying "Two steps forward. One step back." Just accept now, that they are going to come and it will be ok. Also as you can imagine, there is a learning curve when a family has a new baby; no matter how many kids are at home. There is always an adjustment. For our family, there was an even steeper learning curve in learning how to care for myself and the family as a whole. It is incredibly important to give grace and ask for help! This is where our family had to bridge the gaps in our abilities.

Fourth, I would say hold space for all emotions. Too often, way too often, our society says dismissive statements like "Oh, you should not be sad about {insert situation you wanted} because you survived!" For me, the first time I would experience this lovely statement, was when I was sad I couldn't nurse my my baby. It was just over 3 months after we experienced our AFE. I had decided to stop pumping and trying to get my body to produce milk to nourish my baby. A well-meaning family member tried to encourage me but really missed the mark. After their comment, I explained how it's ok for me to be sad I can't nurse my baby AND grateful I survived. Tension between two emotions is possible and, in my opinion, healthy: Grieving and gratitude!

Just remember whatever your hard is, you are capable of hard things. Everyone is.

Connect With Catherine

www.birthtraumastories.com
Podcast- Birth Trauma Stories

YOUR NEEDS MATTER: HOW BOUNDARIES MAKE FOR A BETTER LIFE

Sheryl Green

What do you need?

That's the question Sheryl Green's therapist asked her during their first session. Sheryl just stared at her like a deer in headlights.

"No one has ever asked me that," she said.

If you consider yourself a people-pleaser, struggle with setting boundaries, and find it nearly impossible to say no, there's a good chance no one has ever asked you that question, either.

Why? Because what you needed or wanted never mattered, only what others needed or wanted from you.
Until now.

Welcome to the first day of the rest of your life. Today, you learn that it is not only your right but your responsibility to set healthy boundaries with family, friends, colleagues, bosses, employees, etc.

What Are Boundaries?

Boundaries are how we allow others to treat us and, by extension, our stuff. They are our expectations, and they fall into six categories: Material, Mental, Emotional, Physical, Sexual, and Time. Have you ever had a friend ask to borrow money? If you're a people-pleaser, you probably handed over the cash, even if it left you in a bit of a pickle. After all, you can't say no to a friend, right? Or can you?

Setting healthy boundaries isn't about controlling others, throwing up walls and not letting other people get close, or being a selfish Scrooge who refuses to help anyone.

Muhammad Ali once said, "Service to others is the rent you pay for your room here on earth." And he was right! However, we must ensure that our needs are met so we have the ability to help others. Setting healthy boundaries is finding the line between giving of yourself and giving up yourself.

Why Is It So Important to Set Boundaries?

Here's the tricky part. If you weren't raised in a home where you were taught boundaries, or even worse, raised to believe you weren't allowed to set boundaries, you may not realize just how important they are.

Without boundaries, we feel:

• Exhausted, stressed out, and burned out
• Taken advantage of
• Resentful of the people we love
• Angry (which leads to snapping at people and starting arguments)
• Depressed and hopeless

To sum it up, a lack of boundaries and not speaking up for yourself has the potential to ruin relationships. Setting boundaries and making our needs known, on the other hand, can help us improve our relationships, making them healthier, stronger, and mutually beneficial.

What Will Happen If I Set a Boundary?

Much like most people aren't afraid of heights so much as falling from them, most people who struggle with boundaries aren't afraid of saying No. They are afraid of what will happen if they do.

To be honest, this is a legitimate fear. If you're not comfortable being uncomfortable (more on that in a moment), you may be tempted to backpedal on your response if the other person doesn't receive it well. The trick is to go into boundary conversations knowing what might happen.

The people in your life will fall into three camps.

1. The first group will congratulate you. They've been waiting years for you to learn how to set boundaries and now that you have, they couldn't be prouder.

2. The second group (and this is the majority) will struggle at first. They are used to you being their go-to for absolutely everything, and your No will throw a major wrench in their plans. However, they ultimately love you and want what's best for you. They may try to guilt trip you initially, but if you stand firm, they will accept (and come to love) version You 2.0.

3. The third group (aka Boundary Busters) are the people who want what they want no matter the cost to you. They don't care if you are evolving. They are angry that you won't do whatever it is you've always done for them, and they will throw the adult version of a temper tantrum. This is not your problem. These people will either figure out that this is how things will be from now on, or they will refuse to accept it. If they choose the latter, the ball is in your court. These people do not deserve to be in your life. It can be painful to cut people out, but not nearly as painful as giving in and allowing them to treat you poorly for all time.

Being prepared with this knowledge will help you face boundary conversations with confidence. What does this look like in action?

There was an episode of Young Sheldon in which Sheldon wanted his "**Meemaw**" (Annie Potts crushes this role) to drive him somewhere. Could she have rearranged her schedule and put her own needs on hold, as she often does for him? Yes. Did she want to? Nope. So, she declined, and the conversation that ensued was pure boundary genius.

"***I'm very disappointed,***" said Sheldon.
"***And I'm okay with that,***" Meemaw responded.

Yeah, that's it. If you were expecting some long dialogue here, you may be disappointed. She could have changed her answer to make him happy. Instead, Meemaw showed us that we don't have to bend to other people's wills just to avoid momentary discomfort.

Setting boundaries can be scary at first. Practice in low-risk situations like asking the grocery clerk to pack your bags differently to protect your eggs, or letting the massage therapist know the pressure is too much and you need her to lighten up. If these conversations don't go well at first, there's really no fallout, and you can try again next time.

Then, once you've strengthened your boundary muscles, you can move on to higher-risk situations like talking to family, friends, or colleagues. Keep practicing. These conversations will get easier, and eventually, speaking up for yourself will become second nature.

Conclusion

You have the right to have needs, to express those needs, and to get those needs met. Setting healthy boundaries or expectations around how you want to be treated will not only improve your mental health but will also strengthen your personal and professional relationships.

Happy boundary setting!

Connect With Sheryl

www.SherylGreenSpeaks.com

LET'S GET MOVING TOGETHER!

By Russell Rogers

In our screen-filled world, it's time to shake things up and rediscover the joy of movement! While our gadgets can be super helpful, we all know that feeling when we've been sitting a bit too long. But don't worry – we've got this!

Why Moving Matters: The Amazing Benefits of Walking Moving our bodies isn't just fun – it's a superpower! Let's dive into the incredible ways that regular walks and outdoor activities can transform our lives.

Mood Booster Extraordinaire Walking isn't just about getting from A to B – it's a natural mood elevator! When we move, our bodies release endorphins, those feel-good chemicals that act like nature's antidepressants. But that's not all:

- **Stress Buster**: A brisk walk can help melt away the day's tensions. It's like pressing a reset button for your mind.
- **Anxiety Alleviator**: Regular walking can reduce symptoms of anxiety, helping you feel more calm and centered.
- **Confidence Builder**: As you set and achieve walking goals, you'll feel a sense of accomplishment that can boost your self-esteem.
- **Creativity Catalyst**: Ever noticed how your best ideas come when you're on the move? Walking can unlock your creative potential!

Heart Health Hero Your heart loves it when you walk! Here's why:

- **Cardiovascular Champion**: Regular walking strengthens your heart muscle, making it more efficient at pumping blood.
- **Blood Pressure Balancer**: A daily walk can help keep your blood pressure in check, reducing strain on your heart.
- **Cholesterol Controller**: Walking can help increase your levels of good cholesterol (HDL) while lowering the bad kind (LDL).
- **Diabetes Defense**: Regular walks can help regulate blood sugar levels, which is crucial for preventing and managing type 2 diabetes.

Sleep Superstar Want to sleep like a champ? Walking can help:

- **Natural Sleep Aid**: Regular exercise can help regulate your sleep-wake cycle, making it easier to fall asleep at night.
- **Deep Sleep Promoter**: Walkers often enjoy more restorative deep sleep, waking up feeling refreshed and energized.
- **Insomnia Buster**: If you struggle with sleepless nights, a consistent walking routine might be your ticket to dreamland. Stress Reducer: By lowering stress levels, walking can help quiet that racing mind that keeps you up at night.

Social Connector Walking isn't just a solo activity – it's a great way to connect:

- **Friend Finder**: Join a walking group or invite a buddy along, and watch your social circle grow.
- **Family Bonding**: Family walks are a wonderful way to catch up and stay connected without screens getting in the way.
- **Community Builder**: As you explore your neighborhood on foot, you'll likely meet neighbors and feel more connected to your community.
- **Four-Legged Friends**: If you have a dog, you know that walks are the highlight of their day – and they can be yours too!

MONTHLY COLUMNIST

Nature's Nurture Stepping outside for a walk connects us with the natural world:

- **Vitamin D Boost**: Sunlight helps our bodies produce vitamin D, essential for bone health and immune function.
- **Green Therapy**: Time in nature can reduce stress, improve mood, and even lower blood pressure
- **Seasonal Appreciator**: Walking regularly helps you notice and appreciate the changing seasons.
- **Environmental Awareness**: The more we walk, the more connected we feel to our environment, often leading to more eco-friendly choices.

Brain Booster Walking isn't just good for your body – it's a workout for your brain too:

- **Memory Enhancer**: Regular walks can improve memory and cognitive function.
- **Focus Sharpener**: Physical activity can help improve concentration and attention span.
- **Dementia Defender**: Studies suggest that walking may help reduce the risk of cognitive decline and dementia.
- **Mental Clarity**: A walk can help clear mental fog, allowing for better problem-solving and decision-making.

Weight Management Wonder Walking can be a key player in maintaining a healthy weight:

- Calorie Burner: A brisk walk can burn a surprising number of calories.
- Metabolism Booster: Regular walking can help increase your metabolic rate.
- Appetite Regulator: Walking can help balance hunger hormones, potentially reducing overeating.
- Sustainable Exercise: Unlike extreme diets or intense workouts, walking is something you can stick with long-term.

Longevity Enhancer Want to add years to your life and life to your years? Walk on:

- **Life Extender**: Studies suggest that regular walking can increase life expectancy.
- **Quality of Life Improver**: Walking can help maintain independence and quality of life as we age.
- **Chronic Disease Reducer**: Regular walking may lower the risk of various chronic diseases.

Your Invitation to Move

Ready to join our walking revolution? Here are some fun ways to get started:

- **Step It Up**: Turn everyday moments into move moments! Take the stairs, have walking meetings, or dance while doing chores. Every step counts!
- **Explore Together**: Grab a friend, family member, or furry companion and discover new walking routes. It's amazing what you might find just around the corner!
- **Nature's Playground**: Parks, trails, and beaches are calling your name. Answer with a resounding "Let's go!"
- **Balance is Key**: We're not saying ditch your devices completely – just aim for a healthy mix of screen time and green time.

Remember, this isn't about rules or restrictions. It's about feeling good, having fun, and connecting with the world around us. Whether you're taking your first steps or you're a seasoned walker, you're part of our community! Every journey begins with a single step. So, what do you say? Let's lace up those shoes and move today – and every day!

Join us at **Movetoday365.com**, and let's walk towards a healthier, happier life together!
Russell S Rogers Movetoday365
#WalkWithUs #MoveToday365 #EveryStepCounts

Bone and Muscle Strengthener Walking isn't just cardio – it's strength training too:

- **Bone Density Booster**: Weight-bearing exercise like walking helps maintain strong bones.
- **Muscle Toner**: Walking engages muscles throughout your body, helping to keep them strong and toned.
- **Joint Health**: Regular walking can help improve joint health and reduce the risk of osteoarthritis.
- **Balance Improver**: Walking, especially on varied terrain, can help improve your balance and coordination.

Immune System Supporter Give your immune system a leg up with regular walks:

- **Illness Fighter**: Moderate exercise like walking can boost your immune system, potentially reducing the risk of colds and flu.
- **Inflammation Reducer**: Regular walking may help reduce chronic inflammation in the body.
- **Recovery Aide**: For those recovering from illness or surgery, gentle walking (as approved by a doctor) can aid in the healing process.

Energy Amplifier Feeling sluggish? A walk might be just what you need:

- **Natural Energy Boost**: Regular walking can increase overall energy levels and reduce fatigue.
- **Afternoon Slump Buster**: A quick walk can be more effective than caffeine for beating the mid-day energy dip.
- **Oxygen Optimizer**: Walking increases oxygen flow through the body, helping you feel more alert and energized.

Connect With Russell

www.instagram.com/movetoday365
www.facebook.com/profile.php?id=100093678386343

DR. DAWN MENGE

How do writers create their worlds? It's a question that many have when one of their dreams is to become a writer. How do we put our thoughts down on paper so that others can not only enjoy our words but come away from our writings with a sense of wonder, increased knowledge on a subject and inspiration to create their own works?

I use my real-life adventures to create Queen Vernita's world. Queen Vernita Meets Sir Heathybean the Astronomer was cowritten with my little brother who is an Astronomer/researcher at Jet Propulsion Laboratory. His name came from his nickname when he was little. We called him Heathybean. As a special education teacher, I included two children with disabilities within the story. These children are enjoying their lives and Sir Heathybean is teaching them all about the wonders of the universe. Promoting their abilities is a very important concept within Queen Vernita's books. The following is a recent 5-star review of our multi-award winning book.

Prepare to be transported to a realm where the wonders of the cosmos unfold alongside the heartwarming camaraderie of Queen Vernita and her esteemed guests in Dr. Dawn Menge's enchanting tale!

In the illustrious castle of the land of Oceaneers, Sir Heathy Bean and Cora the Teacher embark on a twelve-month odyssey dedicated to unraveling the mysteries of the solar system. As each month unfurls, readers are invited to join this intrepid trio on a journey of discovery, from the phases of the moon to the celestial dance of the planets.

But beyond the captivating educational journey lies a narrative brimming with warmth, humor, and camaraderie. Dr. Menge's storytelling is as captivating as the night sky itself, weaving a tapestry of adventure that captures the imagination and tugs at the heartstrings. With every turn of the page, readers are drawn deeper into the magic of Queen Vernita's castle, where friendship blossoms and curiosity reigns supreme.

Accompanied by vibrant illustrations that bring the cosmos to life, "Queen Vernita Meets Sir Heathy Bean the Astronomer" is a celebration of curiosity, exploration, and the boundless possibilities of the universe. It's a testament to the power of knowledge and the joy of discovery, reminding us that even the stars are within reach when we dare to dream.

I have recently created a workbook for aspiring authors to help them gather their thoughts and determine where their passions for writing live. Be it poetry, romance, self-help or children's literature. The main focus for bringing your works to the world is how will your words impact the world? The most important part is that you have to begin.
www.landofquailshouse.com

LAND OF QUAILS HOUSE

To help you begin on your writing journey whether it be a journal, poems, romance story, children's book or a mystery I have teamed up with Blu Impressions publishing to create a very unique workshops and events. We will begin our journey in an intimate setting in the beautiful mountains of Wrightwood, Ca. Nestled within the Pine trees in this small mountain community is a breathtaking castle.

This castle features seven beautifully decorated rooms, a breakfast porch, game room, and a hot tub with a full view of the night skies. We will have a private chef who will tantalize our pallets with amazingly prepared meals from her home county of Czechoslovakia along with medicinal messages. If you find your pallet is more interested in local cuisine this will also be available.

Our retreat is designed to help you begin delving into the workbook to explore your writing passion and experiences and express them in writing to share with the world. **www.bluimpressionsevents.com**

Welcome to the Discover Your Writing Passion Retreat, an immersive writing experience designed to unlock your creative potential amidst the breathtaking beauty of Wrightwood, California. Nestled in the serene surroundings of Westwood Castle, this retreat offers a perfect blend of inspiration, relaxation, and productivity.

- **Luxurious Accommodation:** Stay in the enchanting Westwood Castle, surrounded by the stunning natural beauty of California's mountains.
- **Gourmet Meals:** Delight in delicious, chef-prepared meals that cater to all dietary needs.
- **Exclusive Workbooks:** Receive a comprehensive writing workbook to guide your creative process.
- **Personalized Coaching:** Benefit from one-on-one sessions with Dr. Dawn Menge and Lena Payton Webb to hone your skills.
- **50% Off Publishing:** Take advantage of a 50% discount on publishing services with Blu Impressions Publishing after the retreat.
- **Nature Exploration:** Experience the tranquility of nature walks and outdoor writing sessions in the picturesque Wrightwood landscape.

ELIZABETH MEIGS

Elizabeth Meigs: A Journey of Resilience and Transformation

Elizabeth Meigs had a life many envied. Popular, athletic, and musically gifted, she excelled at everything she set her mind to. She was a cheerleader, a multi-sport athlete, and a talented singer-songwriter who was known for her voice, with dreams of making it to Nashville. In the spring of her 8th-grade year, she was cutting a demo tape in a recording studio. But one week into her freshman year of high school, everything changed.

A devastating car accident left Elizabeth with a traumatic brain injury and a survival rate of less than 25%. Her world turned upside down overnight. Waking from a coma, she found herself reduced to the abilities of an infant. She had to relearn how to walk, talk, and perform basic functions. The road to recovery was long and filled with physical, emotional, and mental challenges.

During these difficult years, Elizabeth faced judgment and rejection from those who didn't understand her struggle. The vibrant life she once knew was replaced by pain, heartache, and loss.

She had to learn how to persevere and become resilient. Despite losing her dreams of performing on the Nashville stage, Elizabeth found new strength and purpose in her journey.

For more than 4 years, Elizabeth came home from school multiple days a week, telling her parents she should have died in that car accident,

believing everything would be easier if she were dead. She cried out, asking God why He allowed this to happen to her. In her darkest moments, she received a profound answer from her higher power. The voice in her heart brought her comfort and peace, saying, "I have a plan for you. You can't stop. You have to keep going."

This voice gave her hope. Jeremiah 29:11 says, "For I know the plans I have for you, declares the Lord, plans to prosper you and not to harm you, plans to give you hope and a future." Elizabeth clung to this promise. She had to have faith and believe in the unseen.

Elizabeth realized she couldn't stop because she wouldn't wish her suffering on anyone. She knew she was destined to become the support and inspiration she desperately needed. She didn't know how or when, but she learned that she wasn't ready yet. She needed to become the person she was meant to be to fulfill her calling. But she never gave up because she wouldn't wish her struggles on anyone.

Every night, no matter what happened that day, Elizabeth prayed to God and thanked Him for her life and blessings. She felt alone, with no one who understood what she was dealing with. So she turned to God in her weakness and struggles, and He gave her the strength to keep fighting. She is proof of His unconditional love. When you feel alone, He will lift you up just as He has lifted Elizabeth.

As time went on, she didn't always hear His voice, but the comfort, hope, and peace He delivered in the first 4 years following the accident never left her.

Twelve years after the accident, Elizabeth graduated with a degree in occupational therapy, where she began to see God's plan and her purpose come to fruition. Five years later, she found a church that gave her the platform to share her testimony, providing hope and inspiration to many more people than she ever could have imagined working a regular 9-5 job. Her eyes opened to all the possibilities and ways she could help others on a much larger scale.

During this time, her confidence in her calling grew because God brought individuals into her life who saw her and believed in her. These people helped her grow closer to God. As she touched the lives He placed in her path, she continued to grow into who she needed to be. She became stronger and found a way to grow and evolve through the struggles, becoming UNSTOPPABLE. This is possible for you too. Elizabeth is here today to be His voice, providing HOPE to you just as His voice in her heart got her through high school and got her where she is today.

In recent years, God revealed to Elizabeth that she was chosen to be His messenger, just as He chose Paul in the Bible. Through His grace and mercy, she realized that the strategies she developed during her recovery were not just for her but a way to help bring His freedom and peace to others battling life's storms. These strategies have continued to support her through difficult times as an adult. When she began to write them down, she discovered that modern science has supported their effectiveness in improving mental health for the past 10-15 years (strategies she developed over two decades ago).

This revelation led Elizabeth to develop her Pathway to PEACE Program, designed to help others build a strong foundation for stress management and emotional resilience. She uses biblical promises when she speaks on stage and coaches her clients, helping them build the confidence to chase their dreams and find success, freedom, and peace. This enables them to develop healthy coping strategies, grow through their challenges, and break free from a vicious cycle of chaos and confusion. This allows them to truly heal on the inside, navigate overwhelm, and transform hopelessness into hope for a brighter future.

Elizabeth's mission is guided by the transformative power of hope. Her mission is to empower individuals on their unique wellness journey, fostering Healing that Opens Pathways to Empowerment (H.O.P.E).

Today, Elizabeth is a Transformational Coach who works in virtual group coaching sessions, with 1-1 coaching coming soon, helping others develop their own Pathway to PEACE. She also speaks to groups and organizations at conferences, workshops, and lunch n' learns. Her holistic approach is effective in both personal and professional lives, addressing stress and overwhelm to improve productivity, reduce call-ins, and more. Elizabeth's strategies help individuals pinpoint the causes of their stress, gain clarity, and take actionable steps to grow through these challenges. By fostering resilience and finding their PEACE, her clients can emerge stronger, just as she has done for herself. She believes everyone deserves a life full of joy.

If you're seeking free strategies to kickstart your journey to PEACE and joy, Elizabeth offers a free strategy download, The-Ei-Method, available in the resources tab on ElizabethInspires.com. You can also sign up for the Free Daily Affirmations subscription to help shift your mindset from negative to positive. It's never too late to start fresh. Remember, the dreams on your heart are there for a reason, and you have everything within you to make them a reality.

If you struggle with self-belief, know that Elizabeth Meigs believes in you and knows you have the strength to rise above the noise and chaos. Just as she has overcome her challenges, you too have the power within you to overcome and thrive!

Connect With Elizabeth

www.elizabethinspires.com
www.elizabethinspires.com/subscribe-to-daily-affirmations

RM INFINITE LLC-ONE STOP POSSIBILITIES

Owners: *Amb., Dr. Randi D. Ward, and Dr. Chaudhry Masood Mahmood Bhalli*

As the Company Name implies, RM Infinite is a Multi-Service Business that focuses on serving the individual needs of its clients. The Owners—a Husband and Wife Team---are Experts in the Services offered. The Company offers Great Rates with Flexible, Negotiable Payments if needed. The Primary Headquarters is in Metro-Atlanta, Georgia, with a secondary location in Rawalpindi, Pakistan.

It is the company's passion to help its clients with whatever they need. RM Infinite believes people should be able to fulfill their dreams and works closely with them to make this happen. Their dreams become RM Infinite's dreams.

These are the expert services provided by Randi.

- Book Writing Coaching - Consultations on discovering the author's book themes, fictional story plots, personal stories, nonfiction topics, etc. and guiding the author through the writing process. This is done on an hourly basis; the number of sessions is determined by need and/or progress. Randi's general Fee is $50 to $75 an hour, but special packages can be purchased to reduce the hourly cost.
- Master Editing - Grammar, Content, etc. for Client Books, Magazine Articles, etc.
- Content Editing - As a content editor Randi reads and carefully edit the manuscript with an eye on the completeness, flow, and construction of ideas and stories, working paragraph by paragraph and chapter by chapter. I offer corrections, pointing out incomplete sections and offering constructive advice on smoothing the flow and construction on all content areas.

Copyediting - She meticulously goes through each book/manuscript and finds the spelling, punctuation, run-on sentences, fragments and any other grammar mistakes.

She will do Final Editing if requested. As a Proofreader she takes the printed version of the book after it's been designed and formatted (called a "proof") and gives it a final review before the book goes to print. Since it comes right before publication, proofreading is the last line of defense against errors. Copyeditors catch all the mistakes the author missed, but Proofreaders catch all mistakes the copyeditor missed before the book goes to the printing process.

Editing Fees are determined by the services requested and the total number of words but usually 5 cents a word. For writers on a tight budget, Randi may offer special deals. Being a writer herself, she often considers the financial status of the writer and charges a lower price.

- Ghost Writing for Clients for Magazines, Biographies, etc. Fee based on number of words similar to Editing or upon an agreed price.

Additional Services Provided by Masood include these:
1. Advertising
2. Book Publishing
3. Branding
4. Creative Projects
5. Events
6. Graphic Designs
7. Marketing

8. Motion Graphics
9. Productions (including Documentaries, Infomercials, 3D Animations, TVC etc.
10. Public Relations
11. Translation
12. Complete Travel Solutions, such as National/International Travel, Domestic/Worldwide Tours, Worldwide Immigration/Visa Consultation, and Insurance will also be provided
13. Graphic Designs
14. Marketing
15. Motion Graphics
16. Productions (including Documentaries, Infomercials, 3D Animations, TVC etc.
17. Public Relations

Future Projects: Designing of High-Quality, Elegant, plus Exquisite Handmade for Brides and Ladies with Great Taste will be available for purchase. These are prepared as Made to Order. Their Display will be Launched very Soon in the USA.

Connect with RM Infinite LLC

www.randidward.com
randiteach@yahoo.com
rminfinite1@gmail.com
WhatsApp +1 -470- 534-0072

CONFIDENCE CORNER
By Renee Vee

GOALS: THE GPS FOR LIFE

Have you ever wondered why some people seem to accomplish great things effortlessly, while others seem to struggle their entire lives? Here's the secret that you may or may not be aware of... the people who are accomplishing amazing things in life all have clear, set goals.

Goal setting is an art. It involves crafting a clear and achievable vision for your future. Why should you care about setting goals? Well, my friends, goals are like the GPS for your life. Without them, you're just wandering around like a lost tourist in a foreign city.

Goal setting holds profound significance in shaping our lives and driving personal growth. By establishing clear, specific objectives, we provide ourselves with direction, motivation, and a roadmap for success.

Goal setting is not just about reaching a destination; it's about embracing the journey of self-discovery, growth, and transformation. By setting ambitious yet achievable goals, we unlock our full potential and create a life of purpose, passion, and fulfillment.

Achieving goals provides a sense of accomplishment and fulfillment. Each milestone reached brings us one step closer to our ultimate vision, boosting our confidence and self-esteem along the way. Celebrating our successes reinforces our belief in our abilities and inspires us to set even higher aspirations.

Setting goals gives us clarity about what we want to achieve. It helps us prioritize our efforts and focus our attention on what truly matters, guiding us away from distractions and toward meaningful outcomes. Goals are like that personal cheerleader you never knew you needed. They keep you pumped, motivated, and ready to conquer the world (or at least your to-do list).

The process of setting and striving toward goals cultivates resilience and adaptability. Challenges and setbacks are inevitable on the journey to success, but by setting goals, we develop the mindset and skills to navigate through adversity, learn from our experiences, and emerge stronger and more resilient.

FOUR GUIDELINES FOR SETTING A REACHABLE GOAL:

The goal is **Positive:** Positive goals focus on what you will do, as opposed to what you don't want to do
For example, I want to spend more time with my family vs. I want to stop staying late at work.

The goal is **Important to You:**
The goal needs to be important to you, not to someone else. You should be able to explain why you want to achieve it and why it will make a difference for you.

The goal is **Specific:**
You want to know exactly what you're working toward.

MONTHLY COLUMNIST

The goal is **Under your Control:**
Your efforts will allow you to achieve this goal vs. Something that is out of your control like winning the lottery.

When we set our goals, we want to be very clear about them so that we have the best chance to achieve them. The key to remember is that goals come in all shapes and sizes. Just because it doesn't work for someone else doesn't mean that you can't achieve it. We learn from both their achievements and setbacks, but as we begin to set personal goals, we learn and grow in ways that you did not think possible.

Remember that setting and achieving goals is a journey, not a destination. Embrace the process, stay committed, and you'll be amazed at what you can accomplish!

Connect With Renee
www.linktr.ee/reneevee

THE NECESSITY OF A VEHICLE FOR SINGLE-PARENT FAMILIES:
A PATHWAY TO SUCCESS

Life as a single parent is full of challenges, and one of the most significant is the need for reliable transportation. In many ways, having a vehicle is not just a convenience; it's a lifeline that provides the stability and flexibility needed to juggle work, family, and personal responsibilities. Without a vehicle, the daily struggles of a single parent become even more daunting, affecting not only their mental health but also their ability to achieve success.

The Daily Challenges of Single-Parent Families

For single-parent families, every day can feel like a race against time. Whether it's getting the kids to school, commuting to work, or making it to a doctor's appointment, the ability to move freely is essential. But without a vehicle, each of these tasks becomes a logistical nightmare. Imagine relying on public transportation to drop your child off at daycare, only to find that the bus is running late, and now you're late for work too. Or think about needing to pick up groceries after a long day, but the nearest store is miles away, and there's no direct bus route to get there.

For many single parents, these are daily realities. The lack of a vehicle forces them to spend hours navigating complex public transportation systems or relying on the kindness of friends and family for rides. This constant uncertainty and reliance on others can lead to a deep sense of frustration and helplessness.

The Psychological Toll

The stress of not having a vehicle doesn't just impact daily routines; it takes a significant toll on mental health as well. Single parents already carry the weight of providing for their families on their own, and the added pressure of transportation issues can be overwhelming. The sense of being stuck, of not being able to meet your family's needs on your own, can lead to feelings of inadequacy and failure.

This lack of autonomy is particularly tough because it undermines a single parent's ability to be the independent provider they want to be. When you can't control something as basic as getting to work on time or taking your child to a medical appointment, it's easy to start questioning your own abilities. Over time, these feelings can erode self-esteem, leading to anxiety, depression, and a general sense of defeat.

Social isolation is another consequence of not having a vehicle. When you don't have a way to get around, attending social events, visiting friends and family, or even taking your kids to a park becomes difficult. This isolation can deepen feelings of loneliness and despair, both for the parent and their children.

The Economic Impact

From an economic standpoint, not having a vehicle can be devastating. For single parents, who are often already struggling to make ends meet, the lack of reliable transportation can limit job opportunities and make it difficult to maintain steady employment. Many jobs require employees to have their own transportation, particularly in areas where public transit is scarce. Without a vehicle, single parents may be forced to turn down better-paying jobs or work irregular hours that are harder to manage.

Even if a single parent does secure a job, the inability to reliably commute can lead to job instability. Imagine missing work because the bus didn't show up on time or having to leave early because public transit doesn't run late enough. Employers may not always be sympathetic to these challenges, and this can lead to job loss, further exacerbating financial struggles.

The lack of a vehicle also means higher costs for other essentials. Grocery shopping, for example, becomes more expensive when you're limited to stores within walking distance or those accessible by bus. This often means higher prices and fewer options for fresh, healthy food. Medical appointments, school events, and even simple errands become costly and time-consuming, adding to the financial strain.

Helping Local Single Parents

The Impact on Success and Growth

Success is about more than just surviving day-to-day; it's about growth and the ability to build a better future. For single-parent families, this means having the opportunity to advance in a career, pursue education, and provide enriching experiences for their children. But without a vehicle, these opportunities are severely limited.

Imagine wanting to take a night class to improve your skills or attend a workshop that could lead to a promotion. Without a vehicle, these opportunities might be out of reach. Public transportation often doesn't operate late at night or may not run routes that connect to educational institutions. The same goes for networking events, professional conferences, or even job interviews that could open the door to better employment.

For children in single-parent families, the impact is just as profound. Extracurricular activities, sports, and other enriching experiences often require transportation. Without a vehicle, kids may miss out on these opportunities, which can affect their social development and limit their future prospects. The ability to provide these experiences for their children is a key part of what many single parents strive for, and not having a vehicle makes this much harder.

The Solution: Driving Single Parents Inc.

Understanding these challenges is why I founded Driving Single Parents Inc., a 501(c)3 non-profit organization dedicated to helping single-parent families overcome the obstacles they face by providing reliable transportation. Our mission is to give these families the tools they need to succeed on their own terms, without being dependent on others like a hamster on a wheel.

We've seen firsthand how the gift of a vehicle can transform a family's life. It's not just about having a way to get from point A to point B; it's about restoring a sense of control and independence. It's about empowering parents to pursue better job opportunities, access education, and provide a better life for their children. It's about breaking the cycle of poverty and dependence that so many single-parent families find themselves trapped in.

Making a Difference

In conclusion, having a vehicle is not just a convenience for single-parent families—it's a necessity. The lack of reliable transportation can have a profound impact on mental health, financial stability, and overall success. By providing vehicles to those in need, we can help single-parent families break free from the cycle of dependence and build a brighter future.

If you're interested in getting involved with Driving Single Parents Inc. or would like to donate to our cause, please visit [DrivingSingleParents.org] (www.DrivingSingleParents.org). Your support can make a life-changing difference for families striving to overcome the challenges of single parenthood and achieve lasting success.

DOMINIKA STANIEWICZ

Who Runs the World? A Closer Look at the Power of the Brain

Who runs the world? This question, famously posed by Beyoncé, was answered in her song with "girls." While this makes for a powerful anthem, it doesn't fully capture the truth. The real answer should be "brains." This vital organ, often overlooked, has a profound impact on our lives. It can be the determining factor in whether life is successful or fraught with challenges. Even those with physical disabilities can face immense difficulties if their brain isn't functioning optimally, experiencing issues such as anxiety, depression, overwhelm, PTSD, anger, feelings of inadequacy, and imposter syndrome.

From a young age, society teaches the importance of a balanced diet and regular exercise. However, education about brain health and optimization is often lacking. Fortunately, the same practices of eating well and exercising also benefit the brain.

Consider the universal desire for happiness, wealth, financial abundance, strong relationships, clarity in life, and reduced stress. Even if someone doesn't aspire to all these goals, they likely wish for at least some. So, how can one optimize their brain to achieve these desires?

The process is simple but not easy. People often operate on autopilot, performing daily routines and harboring self-critical thoughts without much awareness. Phrases like "No one wants me," "I'm useless," "I can't do this," "This isn't for me," and "What if..." are common examples of the brain's negative associations based on past experiences. The brain tends to seek confirmation for these beliefs, reinforcing them through a process designed to conserve energy by generalizing and labeling experiences as facts.

The good news is that the brain has the capacity for change and healing. While not everyone can achieve this, it is possible for many. Here are a few simple practices to help optimize brain function:

1. Morning Sunlight Exposure: Spend at least 10 minutes outside in the morning, longer if there's overcast. This helps regulate the circadian rhythm.

2. Hydrate Upon Waking: Drinking a glass of water immediately upon waking can reduce the likelihood of hitting the snooze button.

3. Consistent Sleep Schedule: Aim for at least 7 hours of sleep each night to allow the brain to process the day's information.

4. Avoid Harmful Substances: Stay away from drugs, marijuana, and alcohol.

5. Challenge Negative Thoughts: When faced with extreme or generalized thoughts, ask if they are true, what evidence supports them, and how life would feel without them.

6. Avoid Certain Phrases: Replace "I know" and "I don't know" with "I'll think about it" or "I'm curious – why?" to encourage problem-solving.

7. Engage in Imaginative Thinking: Use all senses to vividly imagine positive outcomes, as the brain responds similarly to imagined and real experiences.

8. Monitor Health Indicators: Ensure bloodwork is in order, particularly markers for inflammation, iron, vitamin D, magnesium, potassium, ferritin, and hormones. Optimizing these can enhance brain function.

9. Study with Focus: Improve retention by studying intensely for 30-40 minutes, followed by a period of deep rest.

10. Avoid Multitasking: Focus on one task at a time to improve efficiency.

11. Special Support for Head Injuries: If you've had a head injury, engage in activities like table tennis or pickleball, learn a new language, and consider using a hyperbaric oxygen chamber (with a doctor's approval).

These are just a few strategies among many that can be tailored to individual needs and goals. Most people are aware of these practices but haven't prioritized them. Optimizing the brain requires conscious effort to reprogram habits and beliefs. Starting with just two new habits can lead to significant improvements in brain function and overall quality of life.

Dominika Staniewicz, M.S.

Encoding Happiness and Success in Your DNA – Your Brain Coach
Speaker, Corporate Trainer, Brain Coach, Elite Neuroencoding Specialist Author of the #1 Kindle release "The Magic of Dreaming Big, Acting Small, and Achieving Success" (available on Amazon)
Social Media: FB/IG @yourbraincoachd
LinkedIn: Dominika Staniewicz

Demystifying Angel Investing – Invest for Change, Reap Financial Rewards, and Increase Your Happiness

Marcia Dawood

In an era where innovation is thriving, angel investing has emerged as a powerful way to fuel new ideas and technologies. But what exactly is angel investing, and how can anyone get involved—even with a modest sum of money? Let's explore the basics, debunk some myths, and highlight how this practice can be both impactful and accessible.

What is Angel Investing?

Angel investing involves individuals providing capital (financial or expertise) to early-stage start-ups in exchange for equity or the promise of future equity. Unlike venture capitalists (VCs), who manage funds from various sources, angel investors use their own money to support start-ups, often during the early and sometimes riskiest phases of development. As Marcia Dawood frequently emphasizes on her podcast "The Angel Next Door," angel investing is "an asset class, just like real estate, gold, or classic cars," but with its unique characteristics and opportunities.

Who Can Be an Angel Investor?

To qualify as an angel investor in the United States, in the traditional sense, individuals must meet specific criteria set by the Securities and Exchange Commission (SEC). An accredited investor is defined as someone who has an annual income of at least $200,000 (or $300,000 if married) or possesses a net worth of at least $1 million, excluding their primary residence. However, recent regulatory changes have introduced more flexible investment opportunities, such as equity crowdfunding with as little as $50, opening doors for many aspiring investors who don't meet the traditional criteria. Dawood, who serves on the SEC's Small Business Capital Formation Advisory Committee, is a vocal advocate for making angel investing accessible to a much broader audience.

The Motivations Behind Angel Investing

Angel investing also gives people the opportunity to work toward making a meaningful impact. Angels often invest not just financial capital but also their time, expertise, and networks, offering guidance and mentorship to these early-stage companies. In her podcast, Dawood highlights how angel investors "help entrepreneurs grow their companies and create jobs," contributing to local economies and fostering innovation in areas that might otherwise be overlooked.

People choose to become angel investors for a variety of reasons. For many, it's a chance to be part of something bigger than themselves, supporting innovative ideas and technologies that have the potential to make a significant impact.

Some are motivated by the desire to give back, using their business acumen to help new entrepreneurs succeed. Dawood's "The Angel Next Door Podcast" frequently features stories from angel investors who share their motivations and experiences, as well as experts who provide valuable insights for listeners interested in this form of investing.

The Importance of Diversity in Angel Investing

Research has shown that diverse teams get better results in various business aspects, including innovation, decision-making, and financial returns. Yet, despite this advantage, the funding landscape remains starkly imbalanced. Women-led startups receive less than 3% of venture capital funding, while Black, Indigenous, and People of Color (BiPOC) founders secure less than 1%.

This lack of funding for diverse founders repres ents not only a social inequity but also a missed opportunity for investors. Diverse teams bring different perspectives and experiences, which can lead to unique solutions and broader market appeal. Angel investors can have a pivotal role in correcting this imbalance by consciously directing their funds toward diverse founders.

The Structure of Angel Groups and Funds

Different types of angels exist, ranging from solo investors to members of angel groups and participants in angel funds. Solo angels invest independently, making their own decisions. However, many opt to join networks or groups, allowing them to pool their expertise and resources, which can lead to more informed and strategic investments. Additionally, angel funds enable investors to diversify by spreading their money across multiple startups, thereby mitigating some of the risks involved.

Understanding the Risks and Rewards

In her book, "Do Good While Doing Well", Dawood emphasizes the importance of understanding the risks associated with angel investing. Unlike public stocks, angel investments are not liquid; investors cannot simply sell their shares whenever they wish. Instead, they must wait for a liquidity event, such as a company being sold or going public, which can take anywhere from five to ten years or more. In some cases, the startup may fail, leading to a total loss of the investment. This illiquidity and high risk are why it's generally advised to invest no more than 5% of one's net worth in such ventures.

However, the rewards can be substantial for those willing to take on these risks.

Successful exits can yield significant returns, sometimes far surpassing traditional investment vehicles. Of course, consulting tax, investing, legal, or accounting advisors before making important financial decisions is a good idea.

The Emotional and Intellectual Rewards

Angel investing can also offer emotional and intellectual rewards. Many angels find great satisfaction in helping to bring new products and services to market, knowing they played a part in the success of a business. This sense of contribution and involvement is often cited as a key motivator for angel investors. The community aspect of angel investing, particularly within angel groups or networks, also provides a sense of belonging and shared purpose that many investors find rewarding.

Exploring New Trends and Opportunities

Dawood's podcast also explores the evolving landscape of angel investing, highlighting new trends and opportunities. For example, the rise of impact investing—investing with the intention of generating social or environmental benefits alongside financial returns—has attracted a new wave of investors interested in making a difference. Crowdfunding platforms have begun to democratize angel investing, allowing people to invest smaller amounts and support causes they are passionate about.

For those interested in exploring angel investing further, Dawood's book, "Do Good While Doing Well," serves as a "why-to" guide that demystifies angel investing for anyone eager to make a difference but unsure how to begin. It also emphasizes the importance of aligning investments with one's values and the positive impact angel investors can have on society.

Conclusion: The Power of Angel Investing

In conclusion, angel investing is not just about potential financial gains. It's about believing in visionary ideas, fostering innovation, and helping build the companies of tomorrow. For those willing to take on the risks, the journey can be as rewarding as the destination, creating change and potentially generating wealth along the way. Whether you're interested in technology, healthcare, green energy, or another sector, angel investing offers a unique opportunity to make a meaningful impact. With the right approach and mindset, many more can become angel investors and contribute to shaping the future.

For more information, visit my website at
www.marciadawood.com

CONNECT WITH MARCIA

www.linkedin.com/in/marciadawood

www.facebook.com/marcia.dawood

www.instagram.com/marciadawood

Transforming Adversity into Empowerment: Entrepreneurial Journey of Sharon D. "Skyy" Chase

Skyy is a seasoned professional with over 25 years of experience dedicated to making a profound impact on the lives of youth, single mothers, and veterans. Her journey is a testament to the belief that all things work together for good, turning trials into triumphs and adversity into empowerment.

Early Dreams and Unexpected Detours

From a young age, dreamed of starting her own business. However, life had different plans. At 19, she got married and soon became a mother to three wonderful children. Her focus shifted from her entrepreneurial aspirations to building a family. Despite the joy her family brought, she couldn't shake off the desire to create something impactful beyond her home.

A Turning Point

After 15 years of marriage, Skyy faced a difficult divorce. With no money and a heavy heart, she left her government job and returned home to raise her children. This period was challenging, but it also marked the beginning of a transformative journey. She realized that every trial she faced provided her with lessons, skills, and perspectives that would later become invaluable.

The Birth of Greater Works Global

One significant turning point came when her husband spread falsehoods about her to their pastor, who she later divorced because of infidelity. However, this adversity became a blessing in disguise. During this time, her pastor asked her to teach a salvation class. Despite having no prior experience in creating a program or curriculum, Skyy embraced the challenge. With prayer and guidance, she developed her first program in the summer of 1996, it was an 8-week program it was truly impactful and transformational for all who participated. It would eventually become her nonprofit organization Greater Works Global.

Greater Works Global was founded to help youth, single mothers, and veterans rewire their thinking from a fixed mindset to a growth-oriented perspective. The nonprofit organization focuses on enabling individuals to see life's possibilities and understand that every experience happens for their good.

Building a Coaching Empire

In addition to Greater Works Global, Skyy has also established a comprehensive coaching academy. This academy houses all the programs she creates, utilizing her strengths, gifts, talents, expertise, education, experiences and skills. The academy offers coaching certifications in 11 areas, including life, business, money, spiritual, divorce, marriage, and relationship coaching. Her flagship program, 'Who Wants to Be a Coach,' is designed to share her extensive knowledge and experience with aspiring coaches.

Innovative Programs and Courses

As a social entrepreneur Skyy continuously develops innovative programs to address various needs in the community. One of her notable initiatives is 'EMERGE,' a program birthed from Hurricane Beryl when in Houston, Texas, 2.2 million people lost power. Skyy designed a course to prepare for future emergencies for individuals on a in low-income areas. Skyy is certified in Hurricane preparedness so this 20-module program includes a credit-building component and aims to provide practical financial education for individuals with little money.

Another significant program is 'Plug Into the Power,' inspired by a spiritual experience during the 7-day power outage. This 20-module course focuses on helping individuals harness their inner power to reach their purpose, destiny, build wealth, and leave a legacy. It reflects Skyy's belief in the importance of personal empowerment and spiritual growth.

Writing and Speaking Engagements

In addition to her nonprofit and coaching work, Skyy is an accomplished author and speaker. She is currently working on a book titled 'The Sales Equation: The New Formula Sales + Sold = Selling,' which aims to revolutionize the sales industry with 20 unique and powerful chapters. Her approach redefines selling using business etiquette based on a method she coined call The Prism Method based on business, science and biblical principles. Skyy has recently started a program to bring back the art of etiquette in honor of her grandmother called "The FM Campbell Etiquette Academy, with a youth chapter called "Raising Royalty" to introduce protocol, discipline and order to the young generation.

Entrepreneurial Ventures

Skyy is always brimming with business ideas and innovations. . Skyy has recently started a program to bring back the art of etiquette in honor of her grandmother called "The FM Campbell Etiquette Academy, with a youth chapter called "Raising Royalty" to introduce protocol, discipline and order to the young generation.

Family and Personal Life

Despite her busy professional life, Skyy values her family deeply. She is a proud grandmother and supports her granddaughter's entrepreneurial ventures. Her granddaughters, at just 15 & 13 Skyy produced, a PSA infomercial, coached them to write their first book causing them to becoming first time authors, and helped them start their own T-shirt business. She also has a 3-year-old granddaughter who is also an author she has her own coloring book line called, "Kai's Kolors. Skyy is leaving a legacy for generations to come.

Faith and Inspiration

Faith plays a central role in Skyy's life. She believes that God speaks to her, providing her with ideas and revelations that guide her path. This spiritual connection inspires her to create programs and courses that have a meaningful impact on others. She finds fulfillment in utilizing God's intelligence, with AI as her assistant, to create dynamic, human, and cutting-edge content.

Looking Forward

As Skyy reflects on her journey, she recognizes that every experience, no matter how challenging, has contributed to her growth and success. Her story is one of resilience, faith, and empowerment. She continues to inspire and empower others through her nonprofit, coaching academy, and various entrepreneurial ventures.

With a heart full of passion and a mind brimming with ideas, Skyy is dedicated to helping individuals realize their potential and embrace the greatness within them. She believes that life is not just happening to us; it is happening for us. Through her work, she aims to transform trials into triumphs and create a legacy of empowerment for future generations.

Connect With Skyy

www.skyychase.com

MOURNING INTO DANCING: A FRESH LOOK AT FUNERALS AND GRIEF

By Jason Harris, Certified Celebrant, Author and Speaker

Ask anyone to join you in a word association game. "Say the first thing that comes to your mind when you hear the words: funeral, graveside, memorial or eulogy." Many people default to rather negative terms: sorrow, depression, sadness, hopelessness, mourning. When certified celebrant, Jason Harris concludes one of his services, he almost always has at least one or more attendees stop him to say, "I have been to many funerals, but I have never seen or heard anything like what I just saw and heard here today." It is also quite common for funeral directors to say of Jason, "We have never heard so much laughter coming out of our chapel than when he does services here." Those are stark differences to how most people remember traditional funerals over the years.

People often think of everyone wearing black, speaking in hushed tones, very serious and sad faces, organ music with heavy tremolo playing in the background and hearing a minister begin in a somber tone, "We are gathered here today..." Think about it. When anyone even says, "I went to a funeral today," the initial response is, "Oh. I'm sorry to hear that." Now, of course, that is the most common reaction, simply because it often means a friend or family member has passed away, causing great sorrow and loss. But why the disparity?

Peoples' attitudes toward funerals have been shaped by how most of society has experienced these services in the past, causing many to come to the conclusion that when they come to the end of their lives, they would just as soon not have a big fuss made over them. Many say things like, "I don't care what you do with me. I'll be dead. Just cremate me. Don't make a fuss." Too often these days, the funeral industry is seen more as a disposal industry. What should we do with the body? But Jason views the funeral service through a different lens: the lens of celebration.

He uses the following illustration, which is apropos with the 2024 Summer Olympics in full swing. He asks, "Have you ever seen an Olympic athlete when gold for his country look over at the judges and say, 'Why don't you just put that gold medal in a box and mail it to me? Here is my address.'?" Of course not. There is a ceremony. That athlete is placed on the highest of three platforms, the medal is hung around his neck, the banner of his country is raised while the anthem is played, and in more cases than not, you will see tears streaming down the face of that athlete. Why? Is he sad because his event is over? Not at all. In fact, he is not sad at all.

He is moved with emotion as he reflects on all the effort that brought him to this place. He hears the roar of the crowd and knows his family and friends are affirming by their cheers and applause, "Look what you did!" Jason often shares that illustration and applies it as he motions toward a casket or urn or portrait, saying, "This is his/her platform. You are his/her banner and anthem. Let's celebrate, because we are not here today because he/she has died; rather, we are here because he/she lived!"

Jason was licensed and ordained as a minister over 35 years ago. When he was a pastor, he was often asked to do funerals when a church member passed away. It is the default choice, as an ordained minister often quips, "I can marry 'em and bury 'em." However, upon reflection upon his eight years of schooling, both in Bible college and earning his Master's degree from a seminary, he had "only one lecture about funerals," which primarily covered protocol, decorum and suggested passages from Scripture that are appropriate to use at such services. His conclusion? Clergy are trained to preach at funerals.

Now, it should be noted that many pastors do, in fact, do an excellent job speaking words of comfort; however, all too often, an obituary is handed to a preacher minutes before a service, which is then read somewhat badly, mispronouncing names at times, then a sermon about heaven is preached. That sounds cliché, perhaps, but Jason believes that a family does not need a sermon as much as they need a celebration.

Jason has been working with funeral homes for about 12 years beginning as a preneed counselor; that is, he helps people prearrange funeral arrangements for the personal, emotional and financial benefits, along with the peace of mind that comes from knowing that if something unexpected happens, the spouse, children or other family members are not left to make arrangements on one of the worst days of their lives. He advanced to a role of management that had him training others to do this all across East Texas, working with over 50 funeral homes and directors. Because of his ministry background, he was once asked if he could speak at a funeral for a family that did not have a church home or a pastor. He agreed, but asked to meet with the family, since he obviously did not know the person who had passed away, because, how could he possibly lead a celebration for someone he did not know in this life? This changed everything.

Jason developed five questions, that, if he could get answered by as many friends and family members as possible, he could write a fitting eulogy that would be more personable. But that was only the beginning. What he soon discovered was that when he worked these responses into the eulogy, the natural response at the service was not only smiles and laughter through the tears (a very healing emotion), but also that it really lent itself to interactive participation from those gathered, which induced even more smiles and laughter.

Jason has further observed that, just as surely as pastors and chaplains are not taught how to do funerals, people, in general, have never been taught how to support grieving people. There is no class in high school or college called, "What to say to someone whose loved one has died." So people are left to glean from the cliches and platitudes they hear across the years from movies, perhaps, or just what they have heard others say in such circumstances. Many times, said platitudes begin with the words "At least..." which almost never lands well. "At least he isn't suffering anymore." "At least she is in a better place." Or things are said like, "Time heals all wounds."

In his groundbreaking book, "Good Grief. Celebrate Your Life," Jason equips anyone who reads it with these "five questions that will change your life" with four significant applications to these questions, as well as challenging the reader how to stay on the journey with those who are grieving, rather than just showing up at the funeral, when they are feeling rather numb.

Jason's passion is public speaking and loves to unpack these truths. Book him today to bring this message to you.

CONNECT WITH JASON

www.10xstageagency.com/jason-harris

Please check out my website and watch the short video: www.speakerjason.com

Contact Number: 214-478-2361
Email: njason.harris@gmail.com

Book link: pagepublishing.com/books/?book=good-grief

Decoding Your Food Allergies: What Your Doctor ISN'T Telling You About Your Food Reactions

Alexis Sams

Your food allergies and intolerances may hold you back on a daily basis, causing you to miss out on the people, places and foods you enjoy most. You're not alone though – 20 million people in the U.S. suffer from food allergies. [1,2]

It's certainly not a club you ever wanted to be a part of, especially since the cost managing food allergies continues to climb. In one of the few studies published on the topic, the overall economic cost of food allergy was estimated at $24.8 billion annually (over $4000 per child). [3]

On top of these statistics, people with food allergies and intolerances are often told by their doctors that their reactions aren't true allergies, even though their symptoms are valid. Often, they urge you to avoid your triggers, causing you to embark on a troubling journey where you may rightfully fear food you don't prepare yourself and limit where you go or who you interact with to stay safe.

What they AREN'T telling you though is the secret to resolving your symptoms and freeing you from the constrictions that these food restrictions create.

5 Things Your Doctor Isn't Telling You About Food Allergies and Intolerances

What you don't know could hold the key to feeling better overall and enjoying a better quality of life. Here are the 5 things doctors seldom, if ever, reveal to their patients when it comes to food allergies.

1. Symptoms can be resolved when treatment focuses on the external factors driving your reactions and not just managing the reactions themselves.

Many people say that there is no cure for food allergies, but I have a different perspective. When you consider food allergies and intolerances as symptoms being driven by an external factor, focus can shift to treating those factors as a lasting solution for symptom relief. Old toxins, infections, and unresolved healing from injuries or surgeries are commonly the factors contributing to food reactions.

2. Normal or negative test results don't mean you don't have an allergy.

Most food allergy sufferers would breathe a sigh of relief to get a positive test result as it seems it would identify the source of their food reactions. But what does it mean if your results are normal or negative? Some are told it means that they simply don't have an allergy or intolerance for what was tested. But there's another possibility; it indicates that the problem isn't with that specific area. For example, if you get a negative blood test, the issue may not be in your blood. You need to dive deeper into your symptoms to find the problem area.

3. An overreactive immune system is not the cause of your food allergies.

Focusing your treatment solely on this area is not the most effective solution. Your organs and the systems in your body don't spontaneously go into dysfunction. They do so in response to external factors that they encounter and can't handle. Consider your trigger foods are like the cherry on top of a sundae that send immune performance over the edge, creating your food reaction symptoms

4. Food allergies, intolerances and sensitivities have one big issue in common.

You may have heard that food allergies, intolerances, and sensitivities are all different. However, they do have one significant issue in common. They are all intertwined with your immune system; the differences are in the type of immune cell or the immune processes that is affected.

The intestines contain roughly 80% of your immune cells and your liver is comprised of roughly 40% of immune cells. As they function to process nutrients and detoxify waste in the body, I believe it's safe to consider that the full spectrum of food reactions involve immune performance, making neither better or worse than the other, and having significant similarities despite their differences.

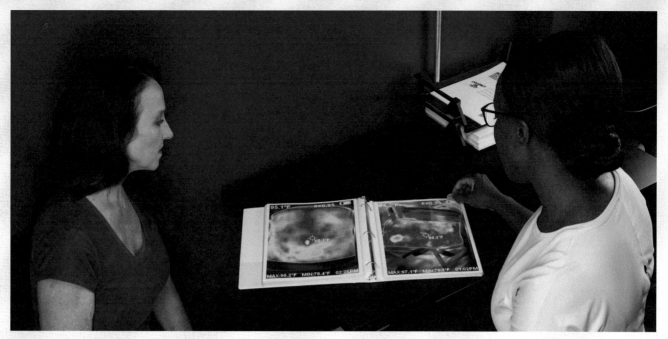

5. Avoiding your food triggers doesn't help your food reactions.

Avoiding food triggers as a treatment for allergies is like ignoring a car's check engine light and hoping that not driving it much will solve the problem. Just as avoiding driving doesn't fix the underlying car issue, avoiding certain foods doesn't address external factors driving your food reactions. In both cases, it's crucial to identify and fix the real problem rather than just sidestepping the symptoms.

It's simply no way to live, which is why you must find the solution. But what can be done if you thought you were already doing what you could to handle food allergies and sensitivities?

Solutions for Reducing Food Reactions

You can reduce your food reactions when you have the right tools and plan to move forward. The process is simple when you follow these steps:

• Identify all external factors that are driving your allergies

• Determine all the organs, systems, and processes being impacted by those factors

• Heal the body from the inside out, according to the natural order of how the human body likes to heal

Leaning this over the years helped me to create The FoodClues™ Approach, which cracks the code on conquering food allergies and intolerances. The characteristics of your trigger foods, along with your food reactions are clues to the external factors driving them. When those factors are addressed and the body receives the support it needs, food reactions subside, all without the need for prescriptions or shots.

For example, people who are allergic to mushrooms often have an underlying mold or fungal infection that drives their reaction. Mushrooms are part of the fungi family, so the reaction to them is a rejection of something the body is already struggling to control.

With a program using FoodClues™, the triggers and reactions you experience from food can help identify the underlying causes and set up a treatment framework to guide your body through the natural steps of cleansing, healing, and restoring to reduce food reactions.

Even though millions of people struggle with these issues, it may still feel lonely when you must constantly make concessions about what you eat. Once you take the power back by investigating your food clues and the external factors behind your food reactions, can open the door to better health and a better quality of life. Simply put, knowing your FoodClues™ is the key to conquering your food allergies and intolerances.

Get your first food clue for free at

www.myfoodclues.com/quiz

3 SECRETS TO HAVE MORE ENERGY

By Krystalore Crews

MONTHLY COLUMNIST

Every day looks a little different, but I know that I will need a nap at some point during the day. Sometimes it's a 20-minute nap, and sometimes it's just 12 minutes! The time doesn't really matter... What's important is giving myself time to rest and recharge so I can go about the rest of my day.

When I need to take a rest, I go through a meditative practice to help me shut my brain down. If you are looking for more energy, check out what I do, then try it for yourself!

I am always on the go! So naturally, people ask me all the time how I can stay so energized, work out, pour into others, and travel... If you are looking for more energy in your life, read on to find out my top 3 secrets!

1. **It's Okay To Take a Break**

   Can I tell you a secret?

   I am not full of energy all the time!

   In fact, sometimes, my brain is mush. With so much going on, it's literally impossible to be at the top of my game, 24/7. So what do I do? I take breaks and allow myself to recharge!

   For example, the other day I was away from home and my typical routine. While I'm away, I still try to keep things as normal as possible. I still wake up, set some daily intentions, eat breakfast, and exercise... But that day, I was completely wiped by 8 am!

   I could have pushed through and kept going about my day. But instead, I listened to my body. I knew that I would be much more productive after I let myself rest... so I took a nap!

My meditative routine

1. First, I set an alarm for the time I need to rest. This can help prevent you from oversleeping. I also turn off all of my phone notifications so I'm not disturbed.
2. Next, I start by relaxing the top of my head. I allow myself to let go of any thoughts and shut down my mind. If you need help doing this, it's a good idea to have a pen and paper nearby so you can jot down any thoughts... These worries can be dealt with once you wake up!
3. Then, I work my way down, relaxing the muscles in my face, jaw, neck, and shoulders. I move all the way down to my fingertips, legs, and toes. I even relax my tongue! During this time, my goal is to focus on relaxing.

I know a 20-minute nap doesn't work for everyone's schedules, and that's okay! You can still take a break and spend some time meditating to recharge and start fresh.

The most important part of this exercise is to not judge yourself... No one can do it all! Allow yourself to take a break so you can tackle the rest of your day refreshed.

2. Stay Hydrated

In my blog post about losing weight, I talked about the importance of staying hydrated... It truly makes such a difference if you are looking for more energy!
Hydration is important for so many reasons. It allows you to have mental clarity and function. It even helps with snacking, food, and sugar cravings because you are more full when you are hydrated!

If you want to set a goal of staying hydrated for more energy, make sure you grab my free 30-day habit tracker! You can use this for any type of habit you want to set, whether it's working out, eating better, or drinking more water... Collecting that data is super important to figure out where you are at and how to reach your goals!

3. Write Down Your Non-Negotiables

There are things that you want or need to do every single day.

For example, in my life, I have five daily non-negotiables.
- I don't miss a meal and eat something every 2 hours
- I need my coffee in the morning
- I need a nap every day
- I need to stay hydrated
- I move my body in some way

If even one of my non-negotiables falls off, my day can go completely wrong!

So what do I do when I need to make sure these are met? I find people to hold me accountable!

No matter where I go, I make it clear that I need these 5 things in my day. It helps me stay accountable to myself, and it gives other people the opportunity to step in if they notice I haven't eaten in a while or need more water. It's so important to notice what your body needs... so make sure you check in with yourself! If you are looking for more energy, sit down and write your non-negotiables! Need some ideas? Check out my list above or join my free health is wealth community over on Facebook for more ideas to boost your energy. These are all great non-negotiables to help you find more energy in your life and feel better every day!

Don't Judge Yourself Not every day will be perfect... and that's okay!

Allow yourself some grace and don't judge yourself if things aren't going right. You can always start fresh by taking a moment to recharge or starting over the next day. And if you want to join a community of like-minded women who can help you stay accountable to your goals while getting fit and feeling amazing, join my Group Fitness Program!

We do hard things together every single week to help you whether you are looking for more energy or simply want to feel better about your life.

Don't forget to subscribe to my new podcast Krystal Clear Life Podcast for more fitness and lifestyle tips!

Connect with Krystalore

www.krystalorecrews.com
www.instagram.com/thecrewscoach
www.facebook.com/krystalore
www.linkedin.com/in/krystalore-crews

Pain as the Pathway

Julie Duncan

Pain points can be the rocket fuel to propel someone to their greatest heights.

-Julie Duncan

Countless modern-day leaders have stories of adversity, challenges, or emotional pain that hits the recesses of their souls.

Tony Robbins, Best Selling Author, Motivational Speaker, Life & Business Strategist and Philanthropist, tells the story of having four fathers. His mother's alcoholism forced him into the role of caregiver for his siblings. Food was scarce. Tony went on to create a partnership with Feeding America, the largest domestic hunger relief organization in the world. Through Tony's efforts, six million meals have been provided to needy individuals and families. His goal is to help one billion people.

Les Brown, Best-Selling Author, and renowned Motivational Speaker filled the Georgia Dome with eighty thousand people after waiting over a decade to begin his speaking career. In school he was labeled as educable mentally retarded: the DT, (dumb twin). His brother, Wes, was the smart twin. Les Brown's speech, It's Not Over Until You Win, is one of the most notoriety events of our time, due to its size and impact upon the world.

Wendy Aimee Porter, founder and CEO of Crowned for Success and Bossladies Mindset, built a dynamic community of over 1.5 million followers on Instagram. She is an award-winning Business and Mindset Coach, a Published Author, and a Public Speaker. Her multi-seven figure business was built following a cancer diagnosis, numerous surgeries, bankruptcy and a leaving a six-figure income in Corporate America. Wendy has collaborated with Tony Robbins, Russell Brunson, and Grant Cardone, to name a few. She has been featured in Forbes and countless magazines and podcasts.

What distinguishes the Tony Robbins', Les Browns and Wendy Aimee Porters of the world from others who are stuck and haven't found their pathway through painful situations? Success leaves clues. These five success strategies are surely embedded in their stories.

"Your past does not equal your future unless you live there."

- Tony Robbins

From Pain to Purpose: Five Pathways

The Movie

Imagine one's life story as a movie. Is it a comedy, tragedy, suspense, or drama film? How did the life experiences impact the main character? Is this a story of bravery or perseverance, leading them to their current state of success and fulfilment? Or is it one of trauma, being a victim of an unfortunate life, letting other judgements keep them from a life of their dreams?

Consider this: One's movie and story create the life they live. It's not the other way around. Yes, the experiences may have been deeply impactful. That isn't in question. However, the life experiences cannot continue to impact one's future unless they continue telling themselves the same story. What one tells themselves going forward is what determines how the story will unfold.

How does the story end? Is the story limiting or empowering? What could be changed to alter the outcome? How could the future story help one to move from pain to living a life of purpose and passion?

Successful people adopt the mindset that they are not what happened to them, rather they are what they choose to become.

"Wake up and start acting like your ideal self. Imagine you're in a movie and you're to play this woman you've always adored. Talk like her. Act like her. Just for 24 hours and see what it does to you."

-Wendy Aimee Porter

Pain or Pleasure

The brain seeks pleasure over pain. Everything one does in life is to avoid pain and move towards pleasure. The overarching goal is turn up the volume on the pleasure factor and turn down the noise of pain. One would do well to compare these two elements. In terms of moving forward what are the emotions? The fears? What is the worst thing that could happen if one pursues their aspirations? What is the pain point of staying where they are?

On the contrary, what impact would there be on one's life if they followed their dreams? Imagine the result. What would life look like in a year, five years, or ten years? What would be the primary feelings of living a life full of passion and purpose?

Successful people weigh the options. Pleasure trumps pain!

Adversity

Adversity is a powerful catalyst for finding one's pathway to success. Often, life coaches have a plethora of adversities, challenges, and even past trauma that they turned into a career to help others heal. Adversity equips people with a deeper level of empathy to understand others struggles. Professional athletes who go on to become coaches have an in-vitro understanding of what it takes to win; the good, the bad and the ugly.

Successful people have a unique perspective on adversity: The battle they thought would defeat them became a tool to PROMOTE THEM.

Mindset

A set back is an opportunity for a comeback In his book, THE COME BACK, TURNING YOUR LIFE AROUND WITH LES BROWN & FRIENDS, Les Brown partnered with fifteen co-authors to illustrate the power of turning one's life around after trying, adversarial times. The stories are a clear illustration of the growth mindset the authors adopted for

success. There are stark differences between a fixed mindset and a growth mindset.

Take Sarah, for example Her parents were laborers and there was a culture of scarcity. Her father abused alcohol and she witnessed a lot of turmoil in her home. Her core beliefs were formed around limitations; she had an internal feeling of never having enough. Sarah suffered from a fixed mindset about her own abilities, as well as the world around her. She settled on a minimum wage job and never lived out her aspirations or dreams.

Emily grew up in a similar situation. She identified with a life of family dysfunction of admittedly was co-dependent as a young adult. However, she saw the turmoil as an opportunity to change the generational pattern. She was determined to move beyond what she experienced as a child. She took steps to get an education, despite her parent's inability to fund it. She sought counseling and worked hard on herself to understand her maladaptive thoughts, beliefs, and patterns. Emily embraced challenges as an opportunity to learn and grow. She went on to live out her dream of being a successful entrepreneur. The differences are clear. One embraced a fixed mindset with insurmountable obstacles and one embraced opportunity for growth.

Successful people cultivate a growth mindset.

Supports

We are the sum product of the five people we spend the most time with. Evaluation of one's social circle and support system are important keys to success. Everyone needs people who are their cheerleaders in times of trouble and times of success. No man is an island. Everyone needs people who provide a safe place, provide emotional support, and help build resiliency.

Successful people invest in reciprocal relationships.

Everyone deserves to live a life of passion and purpose. These strategies can pave the way and lessen the pain along the way.

When life knocks you down, try to land on your back. Because if you can look up, you can get up. Let your reason get you back up.

– Les Brown

IN WHAT WAYS DO YOU LET PEOPLE AT WORK KNOW THEIR CONTRIBUTION AND WORTH?

By Terry Yoffe

MONTHLY COLUMNIST

I'm Terry Yoffe and welcome to the Power of Gratitude.

What are you grateful for today? "I am grateful for _____".

Having gratitude and having the ability to express and acknowledge gratitude is severely underrated in today's busy and challenging world we live in. Being grateful allows us to stay centered, focused and move through life feeling fulfilled and happy for what life has given us and those around us.

Do I hear, "BUT, I didn't get that promotion, raise, new client, etc so what do I have to be grateful for?"

Being grateful for what we do have opens the door to endless possibilities and opportunities awaiting us, even if we don't see them immediately. And, allows us to focus on the positive and abundance, rather than the negative and what we feel we are lacking.

Charles Schwab, Investor and Financial Executive states: "The way to develop the best that is in a person is by appreciation and encouragement".

As a heart centered 2x Certified Executive, Business and Communications Coach, it often surprises me to hear that many of my clients, who are leaders, have a hard time acknowledging those around them and often stop short of letting others know how important their contribution means to the company and to them.

Conversely, I often hear from clients that aren't in top level roles that they don't feel appreciated even though they put in long hours and go the "extra mile" at their jobs.

No matter what role you have in the world of business, letting others know that they are appreciated and they do "make a difference" goes a long way in ensuring work satisfaction and wanting to do the best work for you and your company.

BTW: Having gratitude also applies to our personal life. How many of us remember to be grateful and appreciative to those close to us – family, friends, etc?

When we are grateful for those we love and acknowledge our feelings – eyes light up, tears are shed and everyone feels this connection. HEARTS ARE ON FIRE

If you haven't done so recently, wouldn't this be a good time to tell someone how much they mean to you and how happy you are that they are in your life?

How Can You Offer Gratitude to Others?
• Reach out to your team at work and thank them for the great work that they are doing
• Is there someone on your team that needs that extra boost of gratitude to feel more confident and appreciated?
• What about friends and family members? How many of us take them for granted and just assume we are all fine! Let them know how much you cherish them for being there for you, every day.
• Taking people for granted is a sure way not to feel as connected as you would if you increased your gratitude.
• And, try connecting with your heart and soul rather than your mind and watch your relationships expand and grow 100X over.

Gratitude is one of the most powerful forms of expression, yet we never use it to capacity.

I invite you to stand in the perspective of gratitude and see what comes back to you!
Gratitude is one of the most powerful forms of expression, yet we never use it to capacity.

I invite you to stand in the perspective of gratitude and see what comes back to YOU!!

Terry R. Yoffe – Heart Centered Executive, Business and Communications Coach –
TRY Coaching -- Power of Gratitude

Remember, when you are grateful and full of Gratitude towards others you can achieve purpose and passion and your life can become extraordinary.

If you are gaining insights and embracing the Power of _____ series, I would love to hear from you.

READY TO MONETIZE YOUR INFLUENCE IN Q4? STRUGGLING TO FIGURE OUT YOUR NEXT MOVE?

Are you wanting to close more clients without paying for ads, or marketing? Start here with a strategy call with Bridget Hom, to gain tailored communication strategies to start turning prospects into clients and get into the right business mindset!

Website & Social Media Links:

www.bridgetofreedomcoaching.com

www.bridgethom.me

www.facebook.com/groups/bridgetofreedomcoachingcommunity

THE SCIENCE OF STUCK: WHY CHANGE FEELS IMPOSSIBLE AND HOW TO BREAK FREE

Have you ever had one of those moments where a brilliant idea suddenly strikes you—an idea that could change everything?

Maybe it's a new approach to your health, a fresh start in your career, or a plan to finally tackle that big project you've been putting off. The excitement bubbles up, and for a moment, it feels like nothing can stop you. But then, as quickly as the idea came, your motivation starts to slip away. Doubt creeps in, and you find yourself back in the same place, stuck and frustrated. So, why is it that making changes in our lives can feel so incredibly difficult?

You're not alone in this struggle.

Many of us know what it's like to feel held back, unable to reach the levels of success we know we're capable of. The truth is, there are some very real psychological reasons behind why change is so challenging—and understanding them can help you break free from the patterns that keep you stuck.

WHY WE GET STUCK

Let's start with how our brains work.

Our brains are wired for efficiency, and this often means sticking to what's familiar. Even if the familiar isn't particularly good for us, it feels safe because it's known territory. This is all due to something called neural pathways. Think of these pathways as well-worn trails in a forest. The more you walk the same

trail, the clearer and easier it becomes to follow. Your brain works the same way: the more you repeat a behavior, the stronger that neural pathway becomes, and the harder it is to change direction.

Another key player in keeping us stuck is our brain's desire to avoid pain and seek pleasure.

Change, no matter how positive, introduces uncertainty—and uncertainty can be perceived as a threat. This triggers your brain's stress response, which is designed to keep you safe. Unfortunately, "safe" often means staying in your comfort zone, even if that comfort zone is keeping you from the growth and success you crave.

THE SABOTAGE CYCLE

Now, let's talk about self-sabotage.

This is the voice in your head that whispers (or sometimes shouts) things like, "You're not good enough," "You'll never succeed," or "Why even bother trying?" This inner critic is rooted in fear— fear of failure, fear of the unknown, and sometimes even fear of success. These fears can be so powerful that they stop us in our tracks, keeping us from taking even the smallest steps toward change.

Self-sabotage often shows up as procrastination, perfectionism, or setting goals that are so high they're impossible to achieve.

When we set ourselves up to fail, it becomes a self-fulfilling prophecy. We fail, and then we tell ourselves, "See, I knew I couldn't do it." This cycle can be incredibly hard to break, but it's not impossible.

HOW TO GET UNSTUCK

So, how do you break free from this cycle?

How do you move from feeling stuck to taking meaningful steps toward change? Here are a few strategies that can help:

1.Start with Awareness:
The first step in getting unstuck is to become aware of the patterns that are holding you back. What are the habits or thoughts that keep you in the same place? Once you identify them, you can start to challenge them. For example, if you notice that you always procrastinate when faced with a big task, ask yourself why. What are you avoiding? What fears are coming up?

2. Focus on Small Wins:
Change doesn't have to happen overnight, and in fact, trying to make drastic changes all at once is often a recipe for failure. Instead, focus on small, manageable goals. These "small wins" help to build momentum and create new neural pathways that support positive behavior. Over time, these small successes can lead to significant, lasting change. Remember, progress is progress, no matter how small.

IS MANIFESTING BULLSHIT?

EPISODE 42

WITH CINDY WITTEMAN

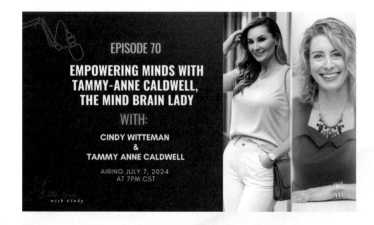

EPISODE 70

EMPOWERING MINDS WITH TAMMY-ANNE CALDWELL, THE MIND BRAIN LADY

WITH:

CINDY WITTEMAN & TAMMY ANNE CALDWELL

AIRING JULY 7, 2024 AT 7PM CST

3. Reframe Your Mindset:
Challenge the negative self-talk that fuels self-sabotage. When that inner critic starts to speak up, reframe the thought into something more empowering. For example, instead of thinking, "I'll never be able to do this," try, "This is challenging, but I'm capable of figuring it out." Over time, this shift in mindset can help reduce the fear and anxiety that often accompany change.

4. Learn to Embrace Discomfort:
Discomfort is a natural part of growth. It's a sign that you're stepping out of your comfort zone and moving toward something new. Instead of avoiding discomfort, learn to embrace it. Remind yourself that the discomfort you feel is temporary, and it's a necessary part of the process. The more you lean into it, the easier it becomes to navigate.

5. Surround Yourself with Support:
Change is hard, but it's even harder when you try to do it alone. Surround yourself with a supportive community that encourages your growth. This could be friends, family, or even a professional coach. Having people who believe in your potential can make a significant difference in your ability to create lasting change. Don't be afraid to ask for help or lean on others when you need it.

MOVING FORWARD

It's important to remember that creating change in your life is a journey, not a destination. There will be setbacks and challenges along the way, but that doesn't mean you're failing. Be patient with yourself, celebrate your small wins, and keep moving forward. Change may be difficult, but it's far from impossible.

By understanding the psychological barriers that keep you stuck and implementing strategies to overcome them, you can start to make progress toward the success you know you're capable of achieving So, the next time you feel that spark of inspiration, don't let it fizzle out. Take a deep breath, acknowledge the fear, and then take that first step. The path to change isn't always easy, but it's always worth it. You've got this.

If you'd like to learn more about how I can help you get unstuck through my Action Mastery Coaching, visit CFViews.com or scan the QR code to schedule a complimentary strategy session.

Strategy Session Link

CFViews.com

Meet Monique S. Pearson: A Multifaceted Leader Making a Difference

Monique S. Pearson is a dynamic force in today's world, embodying the roles of international speaker, author, philanthropist, and CEO of Soaring W/O Limits Enterprises. Her life and career are a testament to her unwavering commitment to servant leadership, a quality she has demonstrated through her honorable service to her country and her continuous efforts to uplift and empower others.

A Legacy of Service and Leadership

Monique's journey of service began in the United States Army, where she served with distinction. Her dedication to her country did not end with her military service; she continues to serve as a civil servant for the Department of Defense. This dual commitment to both military and civilian service underscores her deep-rooted desire to make a positive impact in the world.

A Mission to Elevate, Expand, and Explore

Monique's life mission is to ensure that her impact—her "dash"—is meaningful and far-reaching. She strives to elevate, expand, and explore the mindsets of as many women as possible. Through her various ventures, she provides women with the tools, resources, and support they need to overcome obstacles, embrace new opportunities, and achieve their dreams.

Her work with Soaring W/O Limits Enterprises epitomizes this mission. The organization empowers women through travel and mindset coaching, offering personalized retreats and coaching programs designed to unlock their full potential. By combining professional guidance with enriching experiences, Monique helps women to soar without limits.

Monique's life mission is to ensure that her impact—her "dash"—is meaningful and far-reaching. She strives to elevate, expand, and explore the mindsets of as many women as possible.

Through her various ventures, she provides women with the tools, resources, and support they need to overcome obstacles, embrace new opportunities, and achieve their dreams.

The Triple E Tribe: Empowering Women in Male-Dominated Industries

Most recently, Monique founded an online community to support and uplift women working in male-dominated industries called The Triple E Tribe. The name Triple E stands for Elevate, Expand, Explore—principles that are at the heart of Monique's mission to help women improve their lives mentally, physically, spiritually, and financially.

Based on her years of experience as one of the few women in leadership roles in her profession, Monique is uniquely qualified to provide a vital platform for women in similar positions to network, receive mentorship, and engage in professional development.

By creating a space where women can share their experiences, gain valuable insights, and support one another, Monique is fostering a community of empowered women ready to break through barriers and achieve their full potential.

Philanthropy and Professionista

In addition to her professional endeavors, Monique's philanthropic spirit is evident in her charity organization, Professionista. This initiative provides professional clothing and attire to disadvantaged women, helping them present themselves confidently in professional settings. Beyond clothing, Professionista offers informal mentorship, guiding women as they navigate their careers and personal development.

Monique's dedication to philanthropy has not gone unnoticed. She was honored with the Presidential Lifetime Achievement Award, in recognition of her significant contributions to the betterment of others. This prestigious award highlights Monique's unwavering commitment to her motto: "I am blessed to be a blessing to others."

The Triple E Podcast

Monique's commitment to empowerment extends to her podcast, The Triple E Podcast. This platform provides valuable insights and actionable tips to help women improve their lives mentally, physically, spiritually, and financially. By interviewing thought leaders and sharing their stories, Monique offers her audience practical advice and inspiration to elevate, expand, and explore their own lives.

Connect With Monique

www.instagram.com/moniquesariepearson

TAKE YOUR NEXT BEST STEP

With Molly Smith

Just Start: How Taking the First Step Leads to Clarity

We've all been there—staring at a daunting new goal or project, feeling overwhelmed by the sheer number of steps involved. It's easy to get stuck in this moment, paralyzed by the need to have everything figured out before we even begin. But here's a truth that's worth holding onto: You don't have to know all the steps before you start. Just start.

It's a simple idea, but it can be a game-changer. Too often, we let the fear of the unknown keep us from taking that first crucial step. We worry about not having the perfect plan, or we overthink every possible outcome. The result? We stay exactly where we are—stuck, frustrated, and feeling like we're spinning our wheels. But what if, instead of waiting for clarity before you take action, you flipped the script? What if you embraced the idea that action itself creates clarity?

One of the biggest obstacles to getting started is the belief that we need a flawless, step-by-step plan in place before we can move forward. We convince ourselves that once we have everything mapped out, we'll feel confident enough to start. But in reality, this mindset often leads to analysis paralysis. The more we overthink, the more overwhelming the task becomes.

Here's the thing: no plan is ever going to be perfect. Life is unpredictable, and there will always be variables we can't control. Waiting for the perfect moment or the perfect plan is just a way of postponing progress. The truth is, you don't need to see the entire staircase—you just need to take the first step.

If you're like me, the thought of starting something new can be so overwhelming that you don't even know where to begin. I've been there, and I know how easy it is to get bogged down by all the things you think you need to do it before you can get started. But let me tell you something I've learned along the way: just take the next best step.

You don't need to have all the answers right now. You don't need to know every twist and turn your journey will take. All you need to do is focus on the next best step—the one thing you can do right now that will move you closer to your goal.

There's something almost magical that happens when you start taking action, even if you're unsure about the outcome. As you begin to move forward, things start to fall into place. You gain new insights, you learn from your experiences, and you start to see the path ahead more clearly.

MONTHLY COLUMNIST

In my experience, clarity always follows action. When you start moving, you create momentum, and with that momentum comes a new perspective. Suddenly, what seemed confusing or overwhelming becomes more manageable. You might even find that the steps you thought were so important aren't necessary after all, or that new opportunities arise that you hadn't even considered.

One of the biggest reasons we hesitate to take action is the fear of failure. We worry about making mistakes, about things not going according to plan, or about looking foolish in front of others. But here's the reality: failure is a part of the process. In fact, it's often through our failures that we gain the most valuable insights.

Instead of letting the fear of failure hold you back, reframe it as an opportunity to learn and grow. Every mistake is a stepping stone on the path to success. And the sooner you start taking action, the sooner you'll start learning, adjusting, and moving closer to your goals.

Finally, it's important to remember that every journey is unique, and there's no "right" way to achieve your goals. What works for one person might not work for another, and that's okay. Your path is your own, and it's shaped by the choices you make along the way.

As you finish reading this, I challenge you to think about the one thing you've been putting off because you're waiting for the "right" time or the "perfect" plan. What's the next best step you can take today? It doesn't have to be big or bold—it just needs to move you forward. Take that step, and see how things begin to unfold. Remember, clarity follows action—and the journey to your goals starts with that very first step.

Connect with Molly
www.instagram.com/molly.positivepants
www.linkedin.com/in/molly-smith-24345712
www.youtube.com/@mollypositivepants

JANAE FINLEY

TurningPoint Breast Cancer Rehabilitation, a 501(c)(3) charitable organization, is marking 20 years of providing essential survivorship services designed to enhance the quality of life for breast cancer patients of all backgrounds, including men, facing a myriad of challenges in their respective journeys to a full recovery.

As the only nonprofit organization of its kind in Georgia and throughout the Southeast, TurningPoint holds a special place in my heart as my mother continues her breast cancer journey at the age of 89. Unfortunately, my sister-in-law fought her battle valiantly for three years; however, she passed away when she was only 50. I'm also inspired every day by those remarkable patients and survivors who walk through the doors of our two clinics in Sandy Springs and downtown Atlanta, respectively. They — along with nearly 20,000 women and men in Georgia — are such extraordinary warriors and handle themselves with amazing strength, perseverance and grace.

Jill Binkley, our visionary founder, a two-time breast cancer survivor and physical therapist, established TurningPoint in 2003 as she saw firsthand a significant gap in rehabilitative care available to breast cancer patients. A simple task such as reaching for a plate, combing your hair, lifting a child, or swinging a tennis racket could be challenging, if not impossible. Since its inception, TurningPoint has been steadfast in its commitment to providing specialized and evidence-based rehabilitation services tailored to meet the unique needs of breast cancer patients.

As part of our mission to improve the quality of life for breast cancer patients, our comprehensive approach to rehabilitation includes a range of services: one-on-one customized physical therapy, massage therapy, nutritional counseling, lymphedema screening and management, emotional support, and tailored fitness classes. We believe in addressing the holistic needs of each patient, recognizing that physical, emotional, and psychological well-being are all interconnected aspects of healing.

TurningPoint also focuses on reducing socioeconomic, racial, cultural and geographic barriers to care, so we continue to develop programs on this front. To this end, we have implemented two programs: The Atlanta Initiative and The Georgia Outreach Initiative.

The Atlanta Initiative began as a pilot program in late 2021 that works alongside the community to directly impact underserved black and LGBTQIA+ breast cancer survivors in downtown and south Atlanta. There are considerable short and long-term physical, functional and emotional issues facing all breast cancer patients that impact their quality of life, including limited range of motion, lack of mobility, decreased arm strength, and swollen lymph nodes.

Active engagement in rehabilitation and exercise activities has been shown to drastically reduce these painful issues and, just as importantly, can prevent the recurrence of cancer. Research also documents racial disparity in breast cancer survivorship outcomes for Black and LGBTQIA+ patients due to various barriers to care, including discrimination, lack of accessibility to quality care, as well as socioeconomic, age and geographical constraints.

The Atlanta Initiative utilizes a culturally relevant and community-based approach to reduce these known obstacles and facilitates the expansion of community resources to reach these underserved populations. During our pilot program of the Atlanta Initiative, one of our Atlanta Community

Connect With Janae
www.myturningpoint.org

Meet Jazz Cow: The Animated Rebel Leading a Hilarious Fight Against a World Controlled by Algorithms!

By John Lumgair

In a world where algorithms dictate our every move and digital distractions are the norm, an unlikely hero emerges—a jazz-playing cow ready to challenge the status quo. The hero we didn't know we needed.

Jazz Cow lives in the Bohemian quarter on the fringes of the fictional city of Popp World. This character is set to shake up the status quo in an engaging new animated sitcom. The creators invite viewers to join this offbeat hero as he leads a quirky rebellion against a conformist society. Brought to life by animation director John Lumgair and his talented team, the show offers a whimsical commentary on our tech-addicted society, celebrating individuality, music, and creativity with refreshing sincerity.

Welcome to Popp World, a realm where the rhythm of life is dictated by the whims of Dr. Popp, a powerful tech mogul whose algorithms predict your preferences before you even recognise them. In this world, citizens are entrapped in a monotonous cycle of digital notifications, their desires perpetually catered to by an all-encompassing AI system. The eerie resemblance to our own world is impossible to ignore.

Amidst this technological control, one figure stands resolute against the tide of conformity: Jazz Cow. This saxophone-playing cow is not your typical hero—he is a cow, for a start. He prefers improvising on his saxophone and spending time with his friends to fighting or going on crazy adventures. His street-smart, cultured vibe, and like Humphrey Bogart in Casablanca, it masks a fervent dedication to justice and freedom. What does Jazz Cow fight with? He fights with jazz. So, he is left with no option but to put down his saxophone, poetry books, and chess pieces and face the authoritarian Dr. Popp. Popp aims to make the world cleaner, cheaper, and safer, but in doing so, he relentlessly promotes the latest apps, junk food, and autotuned AI pop singles, and pushes out the vibrant chaos of jazz. Enough is enough! Jazz Cow and his band can't take it any longer! But who are they? Dr. Popp controls the infrastructure, and the Mayor of Popp World is in his pocket.

Jazz Cow's mission is twofold: to preserve the bohemian charm of his neighbourhood and to resist Dr. Popp's vision of a homogenised future. From artisanal bakers and street vendors to fringe theatres, slow food, and second-hand bookshops, every element that makes their world rich and unique is under threat.

These misfits refuse to capitulate, and jazz becomes their weapon of choice in this battle for cultural freedom.

John Lumgair's team brings a wealth of experience from BBC, Channel 4, Disney, Amazon, and Netflix, having worked on shows like Animaniacs, Rick and Morty, Adventure Time, Miranda, Shaun the Sheep, and Captain Underpants. Their project also features a stellar cast of comedy actors and jazz musicians from London's thriving and innovative jazz scene. Much like Jazz Cow's band, this team is their own form of resistance against the flood of sequels and reboots dominating the entertainment landscape.

In a bold move, John Lumgair and his team have chosen to fund their project through Kickstarter, embracing the platform's potential to offer a unique and personal creative journey.

"Making Jazz Cow has been a labour of love," says Lumgair. "Doing it this way means it's our chance to craft something completely original. What makes it even more exciting is that our audience gets to be part of the journey, engaging with us as we bring this vision to life. The response so far has been incredibly positive, with many feeling a deep connection to what we're creating." Where did this idea come from? Lumgair explains: "It was during late-night laughs with friends that Jazz Cow was born. Why are glamorous animals always the stars of cartoons? We asked. Why not a cow? And why not give it the power to play jazz? After all, why does it always have to be fighting skills? That was the birth of the Cow."

It was from those nights of silliness that John and his team started to refine the idea and sketch the initial design of characters and their world. It's more proof that the best ideas can come from the most unexpected moments. In fact, John has spoken in various places

about how creative ideas come to you while thinking about something else. And how it's all about connections between ideas.

Despite the contemporary relevance of its themes, those late nights of laughter were over 20 years ago. For many years, drawings and story ideas gathered dust in a drawer, undergoing periodic redevelopment and even being considered by broadcasters at times. Lumgair, who also manages his film and animation production company Quirky Motion with a focus on storytelling, has won various awards for their work. But this has taken up much of his time. With 2D adult animation becoming immensely popular, the project's themes are now more relevant than ever. It seemed like the right time to revisit Jazz Cow. Sitcom writer James Cary joined the team to refine the script, and character designer Selom Sunu revitalised the character designs, making it the perfect moment to bring this project to life.

The team hopes to raise enough money to make a pilot called "The Sax Heist and the Coltrane Code," about Jazz Cow and his team's mission to rescue his saxophone from a high-security safe deposit box at the heart of Popp World.

To become part of the adventure, visit *JazzCow.co.uk* and *JazzCow.Substack.com* and sign up to be notified when they launch later this year. Embrace the rhythm of rebellion join the cow-powered resistance and come on his quest to defend humans from the machine and have a good laugh along the way.

THE IMPORTANCE OF GETTING BACK TO HEALTHY ROUTINES FOR SENIORS

By Cheryl Field MSN, RN

MONTHLY COLUMNIST

Here we are in October, the month of getting back to routines! It has been a few years since anyone went back to school in my family, but the school buses are a visible reminder that we are in the BACK TO season for many of us. I personally don't go to the gym much in the summer. Traditionally I trade my morning gym time for time in the garden. In the spring when I am carrying large bags of soil, plants, and tools this activity swap might be fairly equal. As the summer draws to an end the only thing I am lifting from the garden are vegetables and weeds, and those are not equivalent to a total body weightlifting day at the gym. I have found myself out of the routine of running and lifting and I have just started getting "back to "those workouts. Summer may have had an impact on the senior members of your family as well. Vacations and summer schedules may mean a time where their favorite YMCA instructor is away, chair yoga classes are canceled and the usual opportunities for senior engagement at monthly committee meetings are canceled. This makes fall the perfect time for seniors to get back to some healthy routines.

Get Back to Routine Movement
As I mentioned you may have allowed summer to give you a pass on routine exercise. The extreme heat nationwide caused many to stay indoors and you may notice that you've declined in your physical ability, or endurance. Have you noticed that activities which used to be effortless are harder? Over the summer the reduced number of steps you took, or the amount of movement that you missed may have caught up to you. You know the old saying USE IT OR LOSE IT! Now that fall is upon us it's good to reconnect with your local gym YMCA or even your online favorite video for exercise. Finding new ways for

movement is always the goal. The types of movement that I want seniors to be doing are walking, carrying a small bottle of water in each hand for some light weight bearing and when appropriate cardiovascular training is great! Have you joined the pickle ball movement?

That's great movement and social engagement too! So, look for things to get back to, your bowling league, your monthly committee meetings, your weekly trip to the grocery store, this routine movement is essential for health.
For those staying closer to home you can get back to the internet! The internet can provide access to diverse movement options and there are many online fitness programs tailored for seniors. Go on, play your favorite music and get moving! Remember these are ideas for your back to routine consideration. Always consult with your health care provider before starting new activities.

Get Back to your Baseline
If you've had any illness or injury which resulted in a decline in your usual movement you might have lost significant functional ability. Take a good inventory of what you are able to do, with which device, or with how much help? Consider a physical therapy program to give you some assistance to regain movement and strength. For seniors over 65 this would require a visit with your physician and a referral to a physical therapist outpatient clinic. Taking action now as we head into the fall season is essential. As a senior care nurse my clients also experience these phases in life where a long illness or new medical condition results in a decline in function. It is easy to accept this new "normal" which can lead to further decline. The sooner you see a change AND act on it the faster and more likely it is that you regain those abilities. I encourage all seniors to speak to your doctor, ask for a referral to an outpatient therapy provider and get back to your baseline! Do not accept these small fluctuations in function to define you! Do it now as we are all in the spirit of getting back to something! Winter is another time where seniors tend to avoid the cold, avoid snow slipping falling and because you're staying indoors and avoiding cold weather activities your muscle mass depletes. So, fall becomes a very important time of year to build back up our muscle mass, and build back up energy, endurance, strength, flexibility and balance.

Get Back to Your Advanced Directives

If it's been a few months or more now is a great time to pull out your advanced directives, review your latest set of instructions and make copies for anyone in your family and any hospital, clinic, or office where you might receive care. Review your past responses and be sure you would answer the same way today. You may want to review those choices with your agent or that person in your family who is going to speak on your behalf and see if they have any questions for you. Time has a way of maturing our thinking around these conversations. This goes right along with the theme of this column, getting back to routines which in and of themselves keep us healthy. This is no exception! In the first part of my book Prepared! A Healthcare Guide for Aging Adults I talk about the critical importance of being ready for a sudden change in health, documenting your instructions is a critical step.

Get Back to Updating Your Medications

Hopefully you keep an updated list of the medications and the over-the-counter supplements you take on a daily, weekly or monthly basis. Now is a wonderful time to pull out that list and make sure it is current. If you are reading this at your doctor's office, or the salon, or waiting in the school pick up line, set a reminder to get back to your medication list and update it! Then share a copy of that list with your spouse, partner, or advocate. If you should experience a sudden change in health and you cannot answer questions, your spouse, partner, advocate should be able to whip out this list and share it with emergency medical professionals. A medication list tells providers a lot of information about your care needs in seconds at a time when every moment counts.

Now you might be MOST excited to get back to new seasons of your favorite show, and as long as you're riding a stationary bike in front of the TV like my 90-year-old Dad does- I approve! Remember, as you see the school buses driving around, that it is time for us all to get back to healthy routines!

For free resources and upcoming events:
www.CheryField.com

THE HEART OF DT-RANCH: WHERE QUALITY AND CARE GO HAND IN HAND

by Dennis Taber

Welcome to DT-Ranch, where our animals aren't just part of our ranch —they're part of our family. As a family-owned and operated ranch, we've dedicated our lives to raising the best quality animals, with a level of care and attention that you won't find anywhere else. Here at DT-Ranch, every day is about more than just running a ranch; it's about living out our passion for animals and sharing that passion with you.

Our Family, Our Ranch

For us, DT-Ranch isn't just a business—it's a way of life. The Taber family has always been deeply connected to the land and the animals that call it home. Over the years, we've worked hard to build a ranch that reflects our values: hard work, respect for nature, and a deep commitment to quality. At the center of it all is Dennis Taber, the heart and soul of DT-Ranch.

Dennis isn't just the owner; he's the one out in the fields every day, feeding our animals by hand, talking to them, and caring for them like they're his own children. He knows every animal by name and understands each of their unique personalities. This personal connection is what makes DT-Ranch special and ensures that our animals aren't just well-cared-for—they're truly loved.

Hand-Fed with Love

One of the things that sets DT-Ranch apart is how we care for our animals. Unlike many ranches where animals are just another part of the operation, our animals are hand-fed daily by Dennis himself. This isn't just about feeding; it's about creating a bond and trust between us and the animals.

When you visit DT-Ranch, you'll see Dennis out there with his bucket of feed, surrounded by animals that aren't just used to him—they adore him. They're calm, tame, and healthy, because they know they're cared for. This daily interaction ensures that our animals are not only physically well but emotionally content, which we believe is just as important.

Our Promise to You

At DT-Ranch, we're not just raising animals—we're building a legacy of quality, care, and family. We're committed to doing things the right way, with respect for our animals, our land, and the traditions that have guided us for generations. When you choose DT-Ranch, you're choosing a ranch that puts the well-being of its animals and the satisfaction of its customers above all else.

For more information, visit **www.DT-Ranch.com** or scan the QR code to visit us online. We look forward to welcoming you to DT-Ranch, where quality and care go hand in hand.

JAY COWAL

Podstarz is based out of Toronto, Ontario Canada and our mission is to provide the podcast community with incredible celebrity and amazing professional guests to help increase downloads and gain social media traction. We often get the question "How are you innovative", the answer to that is simple. When two parties come together on the Podstarz website for an interview booking, the entire interview is done on our website.

The podcaster can still use their preferred method of recording (Zoom, Squadcast, Streamyard etc) but the days of the podcaster emailing the talent a link are over. The podcaster puts their link in when booking the talent and when the interview is about to begin the talent simply clicks the link provided on their Podstarz Dashboard and the two parties are instantly connected.

Podstarz also has a countdown clock during the interview to show both parties how much time they have left to chat, and we provide custom graphics to the podcaster for every interview to put out onto their socials. The Podstarz website also automatically converts time-zones for both parties and reminder emails are sent out regularly to ensure no one forgets about the interview.

Why should the celebrities who have access to a rolodex of VIP friends and talent? Podstarz wants every podcaster to have that same opportunity to help take their podcasts to another level of success and excellence.

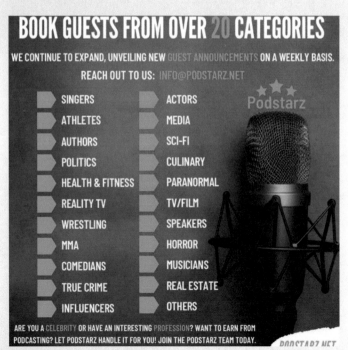

BOOK GUESTS FROM OVER 20 CATEGORIES

WE CONTINUE TO EXPAND, UNVEILING NEW GUEST ANNOUNCEMENTS ON A WEEKLY BASIS.
REACH OUT TO US: INFO@PODSTARZ.NET

- SINGERS
- ATHLETES
- AUTHORS
- POLITICS
- HEALTH & FITNESS
- REALITY TV
- WRESTLING
- MMA
- COMEDIANS
- TRUE CRIME
- INFLUENCERS

- ACTORS
- MEDIA
- SCI-FI
- CULINARY
- PARANORMAL
- TV/FILM
- SPEAKERS
- HORROR
- MUSICIANS
- REAL ESTATE
- OTHERS

ARE YOU A CELEBRITY OR HAVE AN INTERESTING PROFESSION? WANT TO EARN FROM PODCASTING? LET PODSTARZ HANDLE IT FOR YOU! JOIN THE PODSTARZ TEAM TODAY.

PODSTARZ.NET

Connecting The Impossible

Podstarz
www.podstarz.net

- 🌐 www.podstarz.net
- ✉ info@podstarz.net
- 🐦 @PodstarzTeam
- 📷 @Podstarz_Net
- ♪ @PodstarzTeam
- f @Podstarz
- ▶ @Podstarz Team

This Mommy\Daughter trio will share their own life experiences into abundance.

Within this book you will not only find true stories of triumph, but you will also find practical advice you can apply to your own life and circumstances to create the life of your dreams.

Cindy Witteman's growth experience from humble beginnings to become a TV Show Host, the Founder/CEO of a Non-Profit, and Best-Selling Author is as extraordinary as it is motivational. In her chapters, you will read about how she started her life without resources and how she became successful. Was it Manifesting? Was it hard work? Was it complete bullshit?

Kimberley Witteman and Kaitlyn Witteman Chavez were born only 15 months apart, but their stories of struggle and triumph could not be more different. Each have written chapters that draw from their origins and struggles to their individual successes. Although they had a mother who taught them the core tenants of creating a life without limits from an early age, their stories of perseverance will inspire the reader as they forge their own paths from childhood to motherhood.

When Cindy first read about "Manifesting", she wanted to share the concepts with her daughters. Although mom had her own reservations, she told Kimberley and Kaitlyn about a movie she had seen that goes into details and explains a concept known as "Manifesting." The girls watched the movie patiently and left the room thinking their mother had completely lost her mind with this "Manifesting" bullshit.

Fast forward almost 10 years later, they have set and achieved their own goals. They have created their own families and drawn upon the teachings of their mother to form their own individual beliefs and strategies. Now they have all come together as mothers in partnership to write this book and share their journey with the world.

Finally, they will share their own Secrets while they answer the question that so many of us around the world keep asking; "Is Manifesting Bullshit?"

ORDER HERE

Crossword of Champions

Dive into the world of inspiration and motivation with this engaging crossword puzzle. Test your knowledge and get inspired as you uncover words that lift your spirits and drive your ambitions. Perfect for those looking to fuel their passion and stay motivated!

ACROSS

2. The ability to stay focused on a task. (10 letters)

4. The belief in one's ability to succeed. (10 letters)

6. The practice of continuous self-improvement. (6 letters)

8. Represents the ability to stay on course despite challenges. (11 letters)

9. Drives a person to achieve their goals. (10 letters)

10. Someone who inspires others. (6 letters)

DOWN

1. Quality that involves staying positive in tough situations. (10 letters)

3. The act of setting clear objectives. (4 letters)

5. Achieving personal satisfaction and happiness. (11 letters)

7. The process of learning from past mistakes. (10 letters)

Made in the USA
Columbia, SC
31 October 2024

45379373R00040